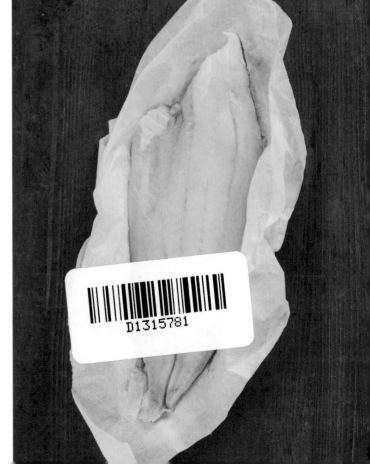

The Clean-Eating KITCHEN

The Clean-Eating KITCHEN

*Feel-good food for
happy and healthy eating*

This edition published by Parragon Books Ltd in 2016 and distributed by

Parragon Inc.
440 Park Avenue South, 13th Floor
New York, NY 10016
www.parragon.com/lovefood

ISBN: 978-1-4748-1761-5

Printed in China

New recipes and food styling by Sara Lewis
Created and produced by Pene Parker and Becca Spry
New recipe photography by Haarala Hamilton

NOTES FOR THE READER

This book uses standard kitchen measuring spoons and cups. All spoon and cup measurements are level unless otherwise indicated. Unless otherwise stated, milk is assumed to be whole, eggs are large, individual fruits and vegetables are medium, pepper is freshly ground black pepper, and salt is table salt. A pinch of salt is calculated as $1/16$ of a teaspoon. Unless otherwise stated, all root vegetables should be peeled prior to using.

The times given are an approximate guide only. Preparation times differ according to the techniques used by different people, and the cooking times may also vary from those given.

Please note that any ingredients stated as being optional are not included in the nutritional values provided. The nutritional values given are approximate and provided as a guideline only, they do not account for individual cooks, scales, and portion sizes. The nutritional values provided are per serving or per item.

While the publisher of the book and the original author(s) of the recipes and other text have made all reasonable efforts to ensure that the information contained in this book is accurate and up to date at the time of publication, anyone reading this book should note the following important points:
* Medical and pharmaceutical knowledge is constantly changing and the author and the publisher cannot and do not guarantee the accuracy or appropriateness of the contents of this book;
* In any event, this book is not intended to be, and should not be relied upon, as a substitute for advice from your healthcare practitioner before making any major dietary changes;
* Food Allergy Disclaimer: The author and the publisher are not responsible for any adverse reactions to the recipes contained herein.
* The statements in this book have not been evaluated by the U.S. Food and Drug Administration. This book is not intended to treat, cure, or prevent any disease.
For the reasons set out above, and to the fullest extent permitted by law, the author and the publisher: (i) cannot and do not accept any legal duty of care or responsibility in relation to the accuracy of appropriateness of the contents of this book, even where expressed as "advice" or using other words to this effect; and (ii) disclaim any liability, loss, damage, or risk that may be claimed or incurred as a consequence—directly or indirectly—of the use and/or application of any of the contents of this book.

CONTENTS

BENEFITS OF
A CLEAN DIET

Clean eating means eating foods in their most natural, whole state, thereby maximizing their nutritional benefits. In the last ten years, the space supermarkets devote to prepared foods in the chilled-food aisles has expanded greatly, and the shelf life of some so-called "fresh" foods has been unnaturally extended, but at what cost? Foods often contain long lists of strange-sounding ingredients that are difficult to pronounce and whose role is unclear. Bread may no longer contain just flour, yeast, sugar, salt, and water; it often includes a number of other ingredients. As increasing evidence emerges about the dangers of eating processed food, clean eating tries to sidestep the problem by going natural.

Clean eating involves eating cleaner, leaner meats and more fish, low-starch vegetables, vitamin-rich fruits, protein-boosting nuts, and mineral-rich seeds. You are encouraged to replace refined carboyhdrates with smart, complex carbs in the form of beans and whole grains, because they take more time to digest, leaving you feeling full for longer while sustaining your blood sugar levels.

Clean eating doesn't mean focusing on calorie restriction; it's about enjoying food as close to "as nature intended" as possible, avoiding refined processed foods and artificial chemicals, flavors and preservatives, and replacing them with foods grown locally, in a sustainable and environmentally friendly way. You are encouraged to eat foods that are ethically produced, for example choosing free-range eggs.

The first step is to look at what you buy and get label-savvy. Food packaging can give a false impression of what is healthy, and phrases such as "whole grain," "reduced-sugar," or "high-fiber" may not tell the whole story, even when they are printed alongside pictures of fresh vegetables, green fields, waterfalls, and well-cared-for livestock. Turn the package over and you may be surprised at what is in the food. Ingredients are listed in order, with those included in the largest amount listed first, and the ingredient you expect to come first may be far down the list. Say "no" to high-fructose corn syrup, hydrogenated oils, mechanically separated chicken, MSG, sodium nitrates, and a high salt content.

Cutting out processed food can feel like a big transition, but as with any dietary change, the hardest part is making the decision. You can still enjoy a burger, just choose a homemade one made with good organic beef (see page 76); it will taste better than the store-bought alternatives. This is a sustainable, proactive approach to healthy living that will see you enjoying what you eat and leave you feeling revitalized.

WHAT YOU CAN EAT

The best way to improve your diet is to start cooking your food from scratch—that way you will know exactly what's in it, including the provenance of the ingredients, and how it has been prepared. Fresh food served straight from the oven should contain no nasty chemicals to enhance its shelf life, especially if you use organic ingredients where possible. You may also be surprised to find that it can save you money, particularly when you have to cook for a family.

CHOOSE WHOLE GRAINS

Whole grains help us to maintain a healthy digestive system and aid good heart health, because the high amounts of soluble fiber help to reduce cholesterol. They are also rich in complex carbohydrates, for a slow and sustained energy release to help reduce tiredness.

Switching from refined white bread to whole wheat is arguably the single best change you can make to your diet. Wheat flour that is sold as "whole wheat" refers to the whole grain that is ground, with nothing taken away during milling, leaving you with 75 percent flour, 23 percent bran, and 2 percent wheat germ. You might also want to try whole-grain spelt or Kamut flour, both of which are ancient varieties of wheat, or brown rice, hemp, quinoa, or buckwheat flour for a gluten-free alternative.

Check the label of any flour carefully. What you think is whole-grain may actually be a mix of refined wheat flour and whole wheat flour, or even solely refined flour with whole seeds, grains, or flakes added. Flour that is labeled "whole wheat" might be refined white flour with 10–15 percent fine or coarse bran put back in after milling.

Wheat is also available in its whole-grain form as wheat berries, which can be used as a nutty-tasting salad base and make a great alternative to brown rice. Also try cracked or bulgur wheat, which cooks in less time than wheat berries and is a great base for Middle Eastern salads. Enjoy whole-grain couscous or whole wheat pasta as a hot side dish in place of white couscous or pasta. Oats are always sold in their whole-grain form, as either rolled oats or instant oats. They are available as groats, which look similar to wheat berries and can be cooked in the same way. Look for barley groats and barley flakes, too. When buying rice, choose whole-grain brown rice or colored rice such as red rice or black wild rice. White rice not only has the fiber removed, but most of the B vitamins are lost in the processing. Also choose whole-grain cornmeal.

FISH AND MEAT

Fish is rich in protein, vitamin B12, which is vital for a healthy nervous system, and iodine, which the thyroid gland needs to function effectively. Oily fish, such as salmon, trout, tuna, sardines, herring, and mackerel, are rich in omega-3 fats, which are thought to have many health benefits, including helping to lower blood pressure. Try to include fish in your diet twice a week, and make one of those servings an oily fish.

Don't be afraid to ask your fish dealer where the fish has come from, how it was caught, and whether it is farmed or wild.

When buying meat and poultry, ask your butcher about its provenance and choose farms with high-quality welfare standards approved by the ASPCA. Look for products with independently certified labels, such as "Certified Humane," "Animal Welfare Approved," "Global Animal Partnersihp," "Food Alliance," or "American Grassfed." Try to have at least two meat-free days per week, and try to keep portions to no more than 5½ ounces per person. Trim the fat off meat before cooking and remove the skin from poultry before eating.

FATS AND OILS

We need fat in the diet to help the body to absorb the fat-soluble vitamins A, D, E, and K and to provide essential fatty acids. The Mediterranean diet, rich in olive oil, has long been considered to be healthy, but there is now a wide range of other cold-pressed oils, such as hemp, avocado, and nut oils, available in some supermarkets.

They are traditionally made without the use of chemicals or solvents, and at temperatures below 104°F, which ensures the full character and essence of the oil is preserved, with natural variations in character and appearance from season to season.

Nearly all cold-pressed oils are a natural source of vitamin E, which is an important cancer-fighting antioxidant, plus they contain essential omega-3 and -6 fatty acids. Many cold-pressed oils, such as flaxseed and walnut oils, keep less well than refined oils, so buy them in small quantities and keep them in a cool place or in the refrigerator.

Butter contains saturated fat, so use it sparingly. Make dips and dressings with yogurt instead of store-bought mayonnaise. The United States Department of Agriculture (USDA) recommends limiting saturated fat intake to as little as possible. They suggest checking food labels and choosing foods with little or no saturated fat.

FRUIT AND VEGETABLES

We are all encouraged to eat five portions of fruit and vegetables every day, but how many of us do this? A medium fruit, such as an apple, pear, or banana, counts as one of your five a day, as does two kiwis or plums or seven strawberries. Potatoes don't count, but sweet potatoes and other starchy vegetables do. While fresh is generally considered best, frozen fruit and vegetables can sometimes contain more vitamins and minerals than fresh, plus they have the benefit of being convenient and are ideal for smoothies and compotes. Canned tomatoes or beans such as red kidney beans or cannellini beans in water make a great pantry standby and count toward your five a day.

Try to choose organically farmed local produce grown by traditional crop rotation methods, using natural pesticides and fertilizers, from your local farmers' market or pick-your-own farm. Some supermarkets also support local producers and will label food accordingly. Alternatively, why not try growing your own? You don't need a large yard; just convert the end of a flower bed or grow salad greens in containers, or have a hanging basket of strawberries by the back door. There's something immensely satisfying about harvesting your own food, and it's a great way to encourage children to be more interested in where their food comes from.

Most pesticides on the surface of fruit and vegetables can be removed with thorough washing. Choose unwaxed lemons, but buy them in small quantities because the wax contains a fungicide to prevent mold growth.

SUGARS

Most of us eat far too much sugar, and with obesity levels rising it is good to review what you eat. Instead of grabbing a chocolate bar packed with chemically derived sugars for a quick fix, go for a homemade cookie with protein-boosting nuts and whole wheat flour and smaller amounts of flavorful dark brown sugar for a more sustained energy boost (see page 116). Most people love moist chocolate brownies, but cut down on refined sugar and fat by adding dried dates (see page 106).

Naturally sweet beets make a surprising addition to a chocolate cake (see page 102), and mean you don't need quite so much butter or sugar. If using sugar, choose types that are as unrefined as possible such as unbleached sugars; natural brown or raw sugars work well, but check the package to make sure the sugars aren't colored after manufacture.

Maple syrup adds a delicate natural sweetness, but again it may not be all that it seems—check the label because some brands are mixed with high-fructose corn syrup. Locally produced honey tastes delicious, and a small spoonful goes a long way.

KEEP IT SIMPLE

This book is all about going back to good, home-cooked meals. Gone are the days of the store-bought meal, the frozen pie crust, or the jar of pasta sauce. However, that doesn't mean dinner will take you an age to prepare and cook, or that you need to go on a cooking course. The recipes in this book are simple, approachable, and made with raw, natural ingredients that are easy to find in your favorite supermarket, health food store, or farmers' market, and they taste great. Here are just some of the problems that switching to clean eating can help you avoid.

HIGH SODIUM INTAKE

Even if you don't add salt, which contains sodium, to your food, you may still be consuming far too much sodium if you eat processed foods, such as breakfast cereals, canned soups, sliced bread, and prepared sauces, not to mention potato chips, peanuts, and other snacks. An excessive intake of sodium increases the risk of high blood pressure, leading to stroke, heart disease, and kidney failure. The USDA recommends that adults should eat no more than 2,400 milligrams of sodium a day, which is 6 grams of salt, or about 1 teaspoon. Most adults eat in excess of nine grams of salt, and the figure is much higher for those who eat a lot of junk food and prepared meals. Every cell in the body needs sodium to regulate fluid balance and maintain healthy blood pressure, but the amount required is small and varies according to age, climate, and physicality.

HIGH FRUCTOSE LEVELS

Health workers fear that the high level of fructose in our diet is set to become as great a problem as our alcohol consumption. We consume over three times more fructose than we did 50 years ago. The liver can usually metabolize the amount of fructose that is found naturally in fruits and vegetables, but it can struggle with the amounts now added to processed foods, particularly in the form of high-fructose corn syrup. Overload the body over a long period of time and the liver may become enlarged. You won't necessarily look fat if you are overconsuming fructose. Avoid sugary processed foods and fruit juices, and carbonated drinks with little or no added nutritional benefit. It is also wise to avoid sweeteners, apart from some plant-base ones.

HIGH TRANS FAT CONSUMPTION

These are naturally found in meat and dairy products, but are also artificially produced to go into some cookies and cakes, with edible oils being industrially hardened to make sure they stay solid at room temperature. It is the artificially made trans fats that should be avoided. Research indicates there is a link between high consumption of these and high cholesterol levels and heart disease.

TAKING STOCK

Forget about using salty bouillon cubes; it's easy to make your own stock. Once it is cooked, let it cool, then pour it into plastic containers or ice cube trays to freeze in handy-size amounts, so that it is ready and waiting when you need it. Just defrost in the microwave in minutes, or in the refrigerator overnight, before use.

VEGETABLE STOCK

Put a quartered onion, with just the outer layer of skin removed, in a medium saucepan. Add three thickly sliced carrots, two thickly sliced celery stalks, two coarsely chopped tomatoes, a bay leaf, two stems of fresh rosemary or thyme, the stems from a small bunch of fresh parsley, and the green tops of two leeks.

Season with a little sea salt and freshly ground black pepper, then pour in 6 cups water. Bring to a boil, then partly cover with a lid and simmer for 1 hour. Let cool, then strain through a strainer.

CHICKEN STOCK

Strip the meat from a carcass left over from a roasted chicken, cover, and chill in the refrigerator. Put the carcass in a large saucepan. Add a quartered onion, with just the outer layer of skin removed, two thickly sliced carrots, two thickly sliced celery stalks, and a handful of fresh herbs.

Season with a little sea salt and freshly ground black pepper, then pour in 6 cups of water, or more if needed to completely cover the carcass. Bring to a boil, then partly cover with a lid and simmer for 1 hour. Let cool, then strain through a strainer.

BREAKFASTS

Healthy breakfast frittata	20
Spinach scrambled eggs with whole-grain rye toast	22
Mushroom and egg cups with whole wheat toast	24
Baked mushroom and herb ricotta	27
Zucchini fritters	28
Buckwheat blinis with pears and blueberries	30
Raw buckwheat and almond porridge	32
Spicy apple oats	35
Cranberry and seed muesli	37
Spelt breakfast rolls with spiced fig conserve	38
Citrus fruit refresher	40
Green jump-start juice	43
Berry kick-start smoothie	44

HEALTHY BREAKFAST FRITTATA

Serve this frittata straight from the pan with homemade whole wheat bread (see page 24), or wrap it in parchment paper and aluminum foil and enjoy it cold at work.

SERVES: 4
PREP: 15 MINS   COOK: 20 MINS

9 ounces baby new potatoes, unpeeled and sliced
2 tablespoons virgin olive oil
4 scallions, thinly sliced
1 zucchini, thinly sliced
4 cups baby spinach, trimmed
large pinch of smoked hot paprika
6 eggs
sea salt and pepper, to taste

1. Bring a saucepan of water to a boil, add the potatoes, and cook for 5 minutes, or until just tender, then drain well.

2. Meanwhile, heat 1 tablespoon of oil in a large ovenproof skillet over medium heat. Add the scallions, zucchini, and potatoes and sauté, stirring and turning the vegetables, for 5 minutes, or until just beginning to brown.

3. Add the spinach and paprika and cook, stirring, for 1–2 minutes, or until the leaves have just wilted.

4. Preheat the broiler to medium–hot. Crack the eggs into a bowl and season with salt and pepper. Beat lightly with a fork until evenly mixed. Pour a little extra oil into the pan, if needed, then pour in the eggs and cook for 5–6 minutes, or until they are almost set and the underside of the frittata is golden brown.

5. Broil the frittata for 3–4 minutes, or until the top is browned and the eggs are set. Cut into wedges and serve.

LOVE LEFTOVERS
If you have leftover cooked new potatoes from last night's dinner in the refrigerator, you can use these instead of uncooked potatoes.

PER SERVING: 241 CALS | 15.1G FAT | 3.5G SAT FAT | 13.7G CARBS | 2.6G SUGARS | 2.9G FIBER | 13.2G PROTEIN | 1.1G SALT

SPINACH SCRAMBLED EGGS WITH WHOLE-GRAIN RYE TOAST

Whole-grain rye bread is packed with fiber, and it has a rich, nutty flavor that complements creamy scrambled eggs perfectly.

SERVES: 4
PREP: 15 MINS   COOK: 15 MINS

4 cups coarsely chopped baby spinach
8 extra-large eggs
3 tablespoons milk
1 tablespoon unsalted butter
4 slices of whole-grain rye bread
pinch of freshly grated nutmeg
sea salt and pepper

1. Put a large skillet over high heat. Add the spinach and cook in the water still clinging to it from washing, stirring, for 1–2 minutes, or until the leaves have just wilted. Transfer it to a strainer and squeeze out as much of the moisture as possible. Keep warm.

2. Crack the eggs into a bowl, add the milk, and season with salt and pepper. Beat lightly with a fork until evenly mixed.

3. Melt the butter in the skillet over medium heat. Pour in the eggs and cook, stirring, for 5–6 minutes, or until they are just beginning to set. Add the spinach and cook, stirring, for 2–3 minutes, or until the eggs are lightly set.

4. Meanwhile, lightly toast the rye bread, then cut each slice in half.

5. Spoon the spinach scramble over the toast, sprinkle with nutmeg, and serve immediately.

THE RIGHT RYE
Be sure to choose whole-grain rye bread.
Check the ingredients list to make sure
no refined flour is included.

PER SERVING: 300 CALS | 19G FAT | 6G SAT FAT | 13G CARBS | 1.5G SUGARS | 3G FIBER | 21G PROTEIN | 1.1G SALT

MUSHROOM AND EGG CUPS WITH WHOLE WHEAT TOAST

Enjoy these baked eggs straight from the oven with hot whole wheat toast and baked tomatoes, or pack in aluminum foil with cherry tomatoes for a breakfast to go.

SERVES: 6
PREP: 20 MINS   COOK: 20 MINS

2 tablespoons virgin olive oil
2 oak-smoked bacon strips,
rind removed, diced
2 cups sliced button mushrooms
3 eggs
½ cup milk
⅓ cup shredded cheddar cheese
1 tablespoon finely snipped fresh chives
12 cherry tomatoes on the vine
sea salt and pepper, to taste
6 slices of homemade whole wheat bread
(see below), to serve

1. Preheat the oven to 375°F. Line the cups of a six-section muffin pan with parchment paper. Heat 1 tablespoon of oil in a small skillet over medium-high heat. Add the bacon and cook for 2–3 minutes, or until just beginning to turn golden. Add the mushrooms and sauté, stirring, for 2 minutes. Spoon the batter into the muffin cups.

2. Crack the eggs into a small bowl, add the milk, cheddar, and chives, and season with salt and pepper. Beat lightly with a fork until evenly mixed, then pour into the cups in the muffin pan. Stir so the bacon and mushrooms are not all on the bottom of the cups. Bake in the center of the oven for 15 minutes.

3. Put the tomatoes on a baking sheet, drizzle with the remaining oil, and sprinkle with salt and pepper. Add to the oven for the last 10 minutes of cooking time. Lightly toast the bread, then cut each slice in half.

4. Lift out the mushroom and egg cups, arrange on plates with the toast and baked tomatoes, and serve immediately.

HOMEMADE BREAD
To make whole wheat bread, follow the Pizza Crust recipe on page 70, doubling the quantities of all the ingredients. Press the risen dough into a greased 9 x 5 x 3-inch loaf pan and sprinkle with 2 tablespoons of rolled oats. Cover with plastic wrap and let rise for 30 minutes. Preheat the oven to 425°F and bake for 25–30 minutes, or until the top is golden and the bottom sounds hollow when tapped. Loosen and let cool on a rack.

PER SERVING: 418 CALS | 18.1G FAT | 4.8G SAT FAT | 49.5G CARBS | 3.7G SUGARS | 7.4G FIBER | 18.8G PROTEIN | 1.9G SALT

BAKED MUSHROOM AND HERB RICOTTA

Ricotta cheese is lower in fat than most cheeses, and is an excellent source of protein and calcium.

SERVES: 4
PREP: 15 MINS   COOK: 15–20 MINS

4 portabello mushrooms
1 tablespoon virgin olive oil
1 shallot, coarsely chopped
1 cup coarsely chopped fresh flat–leaf parsley
1 tablespoon snipped fresh chives
9 ounces ricotta cheese
sea salt and pepper, to taste

1. Preheat the oven to 400°F. Remove the stems from the mushrooms and set aside. Put the mushrooms in a shallow baking dish and brush with the oil.

2. Put the mushroom stems, shallot, parsley, and chives in a food processor and process until finely chopped. Season with salt and pepper.

3. Put the chopped ingredients in a large bowl with the ricotta and stir well.

4. Spoon the herb ricotta onto the mushrooms. Bake for 15–20 minutes, or until tender. Serve immediately.

GOES WELL WITH
Homemade spelt rolls (see page 38), plain or toasted, make a good accompaniment to the mushrooms and soak up the tasty juices.

PER SERVING: 86 CALS | 7G FAT | 3G SAT FAT | 49.5G CARBS | 1G SUGARS | 1.5G FIBER | 5G PROTEIN | 0.1G SALT

ZUCCHINI FRITTERS

Quick to prepare, these fritters make a filling start to the day. Brown rice flour is a nutritious alternative to wheat flour and is gluten-free.

SERVES: 5
PREP: 20 MINS   COOK: 40 MINS

½ cup brown rice flour
1 teaspoon baking powder
2 eggs, beaten
1 cup milk
1 medium–large zucchini
2 tablespoons fresh thyme leaves
1 tablespoon virgin olive oil
sea salt and pepper, to taste

1. Sift the flour and baking powder into a large bowl, then tip the remaining bran in the sifter into the bowl. Make a well in the center. Pour the eggs into the well and, using a wooden spoon, gradually draw in the flour. Slowly pour in the milk, stirring continuously to form a thick batter.

2. Place paper towels on a plate and shred the zucchini over it so the paper absorbs some of the juices. Pat the zucchini dry, then add it and the thyme to the batter, season with salt and pepper, and mix well.

3. Heat the oil in a skillet over medium–high heat. Drop tablespoons of the batter into the pan, leaving a little space between them. Cook in batches for 3–4 minutes on each side, or until golden brown.

4. Line a baking sheet with paper towels. Transfer the fritters to the baking sheet, using a slotted spoon, and let them drain well. Remove the paper towels and keep each batch warm while you make the rest. Allow five fritters per person and serve immediately.

SPICE IT UP
These fritters are delicious with a large pinch of dried crushed red pepper flakes mixed in with the salt and pepper.

PER SERVING: 151 CALS | 6.8G FAT | 2G SAT FAT | 16.6G CARBS | 3.5G SUGARS | 1.3G FIBER | 5.9G PROTEIN | 1.4G SALT

BUCKWHEAT BLINIS WITH PEARS AND BLUEBERRIES

These Russian-style pancakes were traditionally served to mark the coming of spring, and are made with nutritious and nutty-tasting buckwheat flour.

SERVES: 4
PREP: 25 MINS   RISE: 1 HOUR   COOK: 25 MINS

1 1/3 cups buckwheat flour
1/2 teaspoon sea salt
2 teaspoons packed dark brown sugar
1 teaspoon active dry yeast
1/2 cup milk
1/2 cup water
1 tablespoon virgin olive oil

TOPPING

2 tablespoons unsalted butter
2 Bosc pears, cored and thickly sliced
1 cup blueberries
2 tablespoons honey
juice of 1/2 lemon
1 cup plain Greek-style yogurt
pinch of ground cinnamon
1/4 cup toasted unblanched hazelnuts,
coarsely chopped

1. To make the blinis, put the flour, salt, sugar, and yeast into a large bowl and mix well. Put the milk and water into a small saucepan and gently heat until warm, then gradually whisk into the flour until you have a smooth, thick batter.

2. Cover the bowl with a large plate and let rest in a warm place to rise for 40–60 minutes, or until bubbles appear on the surface and the batter is almost doubled in size.

3. Heat half the oil in a large griddle pan or skillet over medium heat. Remove the pan from the heat briefly and wipe away excess oil, using paper towels. Return the pan to the heat and drop tablespoons of the batter into it, leaving a little space between them. Cook for 2–3 minutes, or until the undersides are golden and the tops are beginning to bubble.

4. Turn the blinis over with a spatula and cook for another 1–2 minutes. Transfer them to a baking sheet and keep warm in the oven while you make the rest. Continue wiping the pan with oiled paper towels between cooking batches.

5. To make the topping, melt the butter in a skillet over medium heat. Add the fruit and cook for 2–3 minutes, or until hot. Drizzle with the honey and lemon juice and cook for 1 minute, or until the blueberry juices begin to run.

6. Arrange three blinis on each of four plates and top with spoonfuls of the yogurt, the hot fruit, a little ground cinnamon, and the hazelnuts. Serve immediately.

GLUTEN-FREE FLOUR

Buckwheat flour is ground from a plant related to rhubarb. It is gluten-free, but check the label; it may be milled by machines used for wheat, making it unsuitable for those on a gluten-free diet.

PER SERVING: 437 CALS | 17.4G FAT | 6.6G SAT FAT | 63.8G CARBS | 26.6G SUGARS | 8.5G FIBER | 12.9G PROTEIN | 0.9G SALT

RAW BUCKWHEAT AND ALMOND PORRIDGE

This simple no-cook porridge is a great stand-by breakfast that will keep in the refrigerator for up to three days.

SERVES: 6

SOAK: OVERNIGHT   PREP: 45 MINS   CHILL: 30 MINS

$3/4$ cup unblanched almonds, soaked in cold water overnight
$1^1/4$ cups water
2 cups raw buckwheat groats, soaked in cold water for $1^1/2$ hours
1 teaspoon ground cinnamon
$1/4$ cup light agave nectar
$3/4$ cup hulled and sliced strawberries, to serve

1. To make the almond milk, drain the almonds and transfer to a blender or food processor. Add the water and process for 1–2 minutes, or until they have broken down as much as possible.

2. Line a strainer with cheesecloth and place it over a bowl. Pour the almond milk into the strainer and let drain for 30 minutes. Squeeze through as much of the liquid as possible; you should get about $1^1/4$ cups of almond milk.

3. Rinse the soaked buckwheat well with cold water. Transfer it to a blender or food processor, add the almond milk, cinnamon, and 2 tablespoons of agave nectar and process until slightly coarse. Chill in the refrigerator for at least 30 minutes, or overnight if you have the time.

4. Serve the porridge in small bowls, topped with the strawberries and remaining 2 tablespoons of agave nectar.

ALMOND MILK

Ideal for anyone intolerant of dairy, almond milk makes a great choice for breakfast. Almonds are rich in fiber, vitamins, and minerals, so the milk is nutritious as well as delicious.

PER SERVING: 305 CALS | 7.4G FAT | 0.8G SAT FAT | 55.9G CARBS | 9.8G SUGARS | 8G FIBER | 9.4G PROTEIN | TRACE SALT

SPICY APPLE OATS

Healthy rolled oats get a boost of flavor from apples, dried fruit, and cinnamon in this simple cereal. It can be made the day before eating and stored in the refrigerator overnight.

SERVES: 6
PREP: 30 MINS   COOK: 35 MINS

4 Rome or other red-skinned crisp apples
finely grated zest of 1 unwaxed lemon
and juice of ½ lemon
½ teaspoon virgin olive oil, to grease
2 extra-large eggs
⅔ cup milk
¼ cup firmly packed light brown sugar
1 teaspoon baking powder
½ teaspoon sea salt
½ teaspoon ground cinnamon
2½ cups rolled oats
½ cup dried fruit (raisins, cranberries, cherries, chopped apricots, or a combination)
1 tbsp unsalted butter

1. Peel, core, and coarsely chop two of the apples, then put them in a saucepan. Add the lemon zest and juice, cover, and cook over medium-low heat for 5–10 minutes, or until soft. Mash until smooth, then let cool.

2. Preheat the oven to 375°F. Lightly grease a medium, shallow baking dish with oil. Crack the eggs into a large bowl, add the milk and beat with a fork until evenly mixed. Add the mashed apples, sugar, baking powder, salt, and cinnamon and stir well. Core and dice the remaining two apples, then add them to the mixture with the rolled oats and dried fruit.

3. Spoon the mixture into the prepared dish. Melt the butter in a small saucepan, then drizzle it over the oats. Bake for 25 minutes, or until bubbling. Let cool before serving.

SIMPLY THE BEST OATS

Oats are a whole-grain food and contain protein, the B vitamins, and vitamin E. Their simplicity is their beauty, and their popularity as a breakfast cereal has grown in leaps and bounds in recent years.

PER SERVING: 300 CALS | 8G FAT | 3G SAT FAT | 50G CARBS | 26G SUGARS | 5G FIBER | 9G PROTEIN | 0.7G SALT

CRANBERRY AND SEED MUESLI

A naturally sweetened alternative to store-bought muesli, this nutty and fruity breakfast is bursting with nutrients and so tasty that no one in the family will be able to resist.

SERVES: 6

PREP: 15 MINS   SOAK: 1 HOUR

2 cups rolled oats
½ cup rye flakes
¾ cup coarsely chopped unblanched almonds
⅓ cup dried cranberries
2 tablespoons sunflower seeds
2 tablespoons pumpkin seeds
2 tablespoons flaxseed
2 Fiji, Red Delicious, or other crisp, sweet apples, cored and coarsely grated
1½ cups freshly juiced apple juice, plus extra to serve

1. Put the oats, rye flakes, almonds, cranberries, sunflower seeds, pumpkin seeds, and flaxseed in a large bowl and mix well. Stir in the apples.

2. Add the apple juice, stir, cover, and let soak for 1 hour, or chill in the refrigerator overnight.

3. Spoon the mixture into six serving bowls. Serve with a small pitcher of extra fresh apple juice for pouring over the cereal.

PLAN AHEAD
Mix a large batch of the dry ingredients and store in an airtight container for up to four weeks, ready to add apple and apple juice for serving.

PER SERVING: 330 CALS | 13G FAT | 2G SAT FAT | 36G CARBS | 14G SUGARS | 8G FIBER | 9G PROTEIN | TRACE SALT

SPELT BREAKFAST ROLLS WITH SPICED FIG CONSERVE

What could be nicer than starting the day with home-baked bread?
This quick-cook fig conserve is a great way to make your own spread at home, too.

MAKES: 16 ROLLS AND 2 CUPS OF CONSERVE
PREP: 45 MINS   RISE: OVERNIGHT PLUS 50 MINS
COOK: 45 MINS

4 cups whole-grain spelt flour,
plus extra to dust
1 tablespoon packed dark brown sugar
1 teaspoon sea salt
2 teaspoons active dry yeast
2 tablespoons sesame seeds, plus extra to sprinkle
2 tablespoons sunflower seeds, plus extra to sprinkle
2 tablespoons flaxseed, plus extra to sprinkle
2 tablespoons virgin olive oil, plus extra to grease
1¼–1½ cups warm water
1 teaspoon milk, to glaze
unsalted butter, to serve

SPICED FIG CONSERVE

1 cup diced dried figs
3 small McIntosh, Gala, or other sweet, crisp apples,
peeled, quartered, cored, and diced
finely grated zest and juice of 1 orange
1 tablespoon packed light brown sugar
¼ teaspoon ground allspice
1 cup water

1. Put the flour, dark brown sugar, and salt in a bowl and mix well. Stir in the yeast, sesame seeds, sunflower seeds, and flaxseed. Add the oil, then gradually mix in enough warm water to create a soft dough, at first using a wooden spoon, then squeezing together with your hands.

2. Dust a work surface with spelt flour, then knead the dough for 5 minutes. Return it to the bowl, cover with lightly oiled plastic wrap, and let rise overnight in the refrigerator.

3. Meanwhile, to make the spiced fig conserve, put the dried figs, apples, orange zest and juice, light brown sugar, allspice, and water into a saucepan. Cover and simmer over medium heat, stirring from time to time, for 30 minutes, or until thick. Let cool. Spoon the conserve into a sterilized jar, then leave until completely cold. Store in the refrigerator for up to ten days.

4. Line two baking sheets with parchment paper. Dust a work surface with more spelt flour. Knead the dough briefly, then cut it into 16 pieces. Roll each piece into a ball, put one ball in the center of each baking sheet, then arrange the others around it, leaving a little space between them.

5. Cover each baking sheet of rolls with lightly oiled plastic wrap and let rise in a warm place for 40–50 minutes. Preheat the oven to 425°F. Remove the plastic wrap, brush the rolls with the milk, and sprinkle with the remaining seeds. Bake for 15 minutes, or until the rolls are browned and sound hollow when tapped underneath. Serve with butter and the conserve.

TO STERILIZE JARS
Sterilize the jar in a dishwasher.
Follow USDA guidelines for heating
in a hot water bath for longer storage.

PER ROLL (NO CONSERVE): 199 CALS | 4.4G FAT | 0.5G SAT FAT | 37.5G CARBS | 13.5G SUGARS | 6G FIBER | 6G PROTEIN | 0.4G SALT

CITRUS FRUIT REFRESHER

You can quickly put this together in the morning, or make it the night before and chill it in the refrigerator in a sealed plastic container so it's ready and waiting for you.

SERVES: 4
PREP: 20 MINS

1 ruby grapefruit
1 pink grapefruit
2 oranges
1 honeydew melon, halved, seeded, peeled, and cut into chunks
finely grated zest and juice of 1 lime
½ cup finely shredded fresh mint
2 tablespoons honey

1. Cut the peel and pith away from the grapefruits and oranges with a small serrated knife. Hold one of the fruits above a bowl and cut between the membranes to release the segments. Squeeze the juice from the membranes into the bowl. Continue until the fruits have all been segmented.

2. Add the melon, lime zest and juice, and half the mint. Drizzle with the honey, then gently stir with a large spoon. Decorate with the remaining mint and serve.

GROWING MINT
Mint is such a prolific herb that just one packet of seeds in a large flowerpot will usually provide enough for the whole summer.

PER SERVING: 170 CALS | 0.5G FAT | 0.1G SAT FAT | 43.6G CARBS | 35G SUGARS | 4.9G FIBER | 2.3G PROTEIN | TRACE SALT

GREEN JUMP-START JUICE

If you like spinach soup, you will love this juice. You don't get a huge amount of juice from the leaves, but what you do get is concentrated with antioxidants, minerals, and vitamins.

SERVES: 1
PREP: 10 MINS

2 cups baby spinach
1 cup watercress
1 zucchini, halved
2 red-skinned sweet, crisp apples, halved
1 teaspoon wheatgrass powder (optional)
small handful of ice (optional)

1. Feed the spinach and watercress, then the zucchini and apples, through a juicer.

2. Stir in the wheatgrass powder, if using. Fill a glass halfway with ice, if using, pour in the juice and serve immediately.

NUTRIENT BOOST
Most of us don't eat enough green vegetables and this juice is an easy way to increase your consumption. Add to that the highly nutritious wheatgrass powder and you have a great jump start.

PER SERVING: 223 CALS | 1.3G FAT | TRACE SAT FAT | 51.4G CARBS | 35.6G SUGARS | 1G FIBER | 6.4G PROTEIN | 0.1G SALT

Breakfasts

BERRY KICK-START SMOOTHIE

*This energizing, gorgeous-looking smoothie is a delicious
and healthy way to kick start your day.*

SERVES: 2
PREP: 10 MINS

1¼ cups blueberries
1¼ cups cranberries
⅔ cup plain yogurt
2 teaspoon honey
¼ cup cold water

1. Put the blueberries and cranberries into a blender and process until smooth.

2. Add the yogurt, honey, and water and process again. Pour into a glass and serve.

THE BUZZ ABOUT HONEY
Honey supplies energy in the form of simple carbohydrates, and is a mixture of fructose and glucose. Sweet foods stimulate the brain to produce endorphins, the body's natural painkillers. Agave syrup, brown rice syrup, and date syrup can all be used instead of honey. Agave syrup is naturally sweeter than honey. Brown rice syrup has a mild caramel flavor and tastes similar to maple syrup. Date syrup is a thick, concentrated puree of lightly cooked dates; you can make it by gently simmering dates with a little water, cinnamon, and vanilla, then pureeing.

PER SERVING: 288 CALS | 5.6G FAT | 3.1G SAT FAT | 57.9G CARBS | 40.5G SUGARS | 9.5G FIBER | 6.9G PROTEIN | 0.1G SALT

LUNCHES AND SNACKS

PEA SOUP

*This simplest of soups is bursting with fresh summer flavor,
and the salty blue cheese complements the sweet peas.*

SERVES: 4
PREP: 20 MINS   COOK: 25 MINS

3 tablespoons unsalted butter
2 shallots, finely chopped
4¼ cups homemade vegetable
stock (see page 16)
2⅔ cups shelled peas
¼ cup crème fraîche or sour cream
sea salt and pepper
3 ounces blue cheese, such as Roquefort,
crumbled, to serve

CROUTONS

2 slices of homemade whole wheat bread
(see page 24), cut into cubes
2 tablespoons virgin olive oil

1. To make the croutons, preheat the oven to 300°F. Toss the bread with the oil and sprinkle with ½ teaspoon of salt and ½ teaspoon of pepper. Arrange the cubes on a baking sheet in a single layer, then bake for 25 minutes.

2. Meanwhile, to make the soup, melt the butter in a large saucepan over medium heat. Add the shallots and sauté, stirring, for 2–3 minutes, or until soft. Add the stock and peas, season with salt and pepper, then bring to a boil. Simmer for 15–20 minutes, or until the peas are tender.

3. Strain the peas through a strainer and reserve the cooking liquid. Transfer the peas to a food processor or blender and process into a puree, then return the mixture to the pan. Gradually stir in the cooking liquid until you have your desired consistency.

4. Reheat the soup. Stir in the crème fraîche or sour cream and adjust the seasoning. Serve immediately, with the croutons and blue cheese sprinkled over the soup.

PEAS PLEASE
Green peas are loaded with antioxidants
and anti-inflammatory nutrients, which makes
them excellent for good health.

PER SERVING: 343 CALS | 22.6G FAT | 12G SAT FAT | 22.8G CARBS | 7.5G SUGARS | 6G FIBER | 11.8G PROTEIN | 3.7G SALT

ROASTED TOMATO SOUP

If you can't find plum tomatoes, choose whatever variety you have available for this soup, but home grown are best, of course!

SERVES: 4

PREP: 25 MINS   COOK: 1¾ HOUR

20 plum tomatoes (about 3 pounds), halved
1 red onion, coarsely chopped
6 garlic cloves
¼ cup virgin olive oil
6 sprigs of fresh thyme, plus extra to garnish
4 cups homemade vegetable stock (see page 16)
juice of ½ lemon
sea salt and pepper, to taste

CHEESE CROUTONS
3½ slices of homemade whole wheat bread
(see page 24), cut into cubes
¼ cup finely grated Parmesan cheese

1. Preheat the oven to 325°F. Arrange the tomatoes, red onion, and garlic on a large baking sheet in a single layer, placing the tomatoes cut side up. Sprinkle with 2 tablespoons of oil, ½ teaspoon of salt, 1 teaspoon of pepper, and the thyme. Roast for 45 minutes, or until soft.

2. To make the cheese croutons, reduce the oven temperature to 300°F. Toss the bread with the remaining oil and sprinkle with ½ teaspoon of salt and ½ teaspoon of pepper. Arrange the cubes on a baking sheet in a single layer, then bake for 25 minutes. Sprinkle with the cheese and bake for an additional 5 minutes, or until the cheese is beginning to brown.

3. Put the tomato-and-onion mixture and the stock in a blender or food processor and process to a puree, in batches, if necessary.

4. Pour the soup into a large saucepan and bring to a boil over high heat. Reduce the heat to medium and simmer, stirring occasionally, for 15 minutes. Just before serving, stir in the lemon juice. Serve immediately, with the croutons and thyme sprinkled over the soup.

ALLIUM ANYONE?
Onion and garlic are both natural antibiotics, which means this soup is a good choice if you have an infection, such as a cold.

PER SERVING: 315 CALS | 21.9G FAT | 2G SAT FAT | 25.6G CARBS | 7.6G SUGARS | 4.3G FIBER | 5.8G PROTEIN | 1.6G SALT

FAVA BEAN AND MINT HUMMUS WITH VEGETABLE STICKS

This summery hummus, made with freshly shelled fava beans flavored with chopped garden herbs and lemon juice, is delicious on warm homemade pita bread.

SERVES: 4

PREP: 25 MINS   COOK: 10 MINS

2⅓ cups shelled fava beans
2 tablespoons virgin olive oil
1 teaspoon cumin seeds, crushed
3 scallions, thinly sliced
2 garlic cloves, finely chopped
½ cup fresh mint, torn into pieces
½ cup finely chopped fresh flat–leaf parsley
juice of 1 lemon
⅓ cup Greek–style plain yogurt
sea salt and pepper

TO SERVE
1 red and 1 yellow bell pepper, seeded
and cut into strips
4 celery stalks, cut into strips
½ cucumber, halved, seeded, and cut into strips
1 serving of pita bread (see page 72),
cut into strips (optional)

1. Fill the bottom of a steamer halfway with water, bring to a boil, then put the beans in the steamer top, cover with a lid, and steam for 10 minutes, or until tender.

2. Meanwhile, heat the oil in a skillet over medium heat. Add the cumin, scallions, and garlic and cook for 2 minutes, or until the scallions are softened.

3. Put the beans in a food processor or blender, add the scallion mixture, herbs, lemon juice, and yogurt, and season with a little salt and pepper. Process to a coarse puree, then spoon into a dish set on a large plate.

4. Arrange the vegetable strips around the hummus and serve with the pita bread, if using.

WEIGHING BEANS
As a rough guide you will need to buy about 1 pound 10 ounces fava beans in their pods to get about 2⅓ cups when shelled.

PER SERVING: 446 CALS | 13.7G FAT | 2.5G SAT FAT | 67.7G CARBS | 8.4G SUGARS | 15.5G FIBER | 19.1G PROTEIN | 2.3G SALT

ROOT VEGETABLE CHIPS
WITH HERBED YOGURT DIP

Making your own vegetables chips is surprisingly easy and you can be sure there won't be any added artificial flavorings or preservatives.

SERVES: 4
PREP: 30 MINS   COOK: 16 MINS   COOL: 15 MINS

2¼ pounds mixed root vegetables, such as carrots, parsnips or sweet potatoes, and golden beets, thinly sliced
¼ cup virgin olive oil
sea salt and pepper, to taste

HERBED GARLIC DIP
1 cup Greek–style plain yogurt
2 garlic cloves, finely chopped
¼ cup finely chopped fresh herbs, such as flat–leaf parsley, chives, basil, and oregano

1. Preheat the oven to 400°F. To make the herbed garlic dip, spoon the yogurt into a small bowl, then stir in the garlic and herbs and season with salt and pepper. Cover and chill in the refrigerator.

2. Put the vegetables in a large bowl. Slowly drizzle with the oil, gently turning the vegetables as you work, until they are all coated.

3. Arrange the vegetables over three baking sheets in a single layer, then season with salt and pepper. Bake for 8–10 minutes, then check—the slices in the corners of the baking sheets will cook more quickly, so transfer any that are crisp and golden to a wire rack. Cook the rest for an additional 2–3 minutes, then transfer any more cooked chips to the wire rack. Cook the remaining slices for another 2–3 minutes, if needed, then transfer to the wire rack and let cool.

4. Arrange the vegetable chips in a bowl and spoon the dip into a smaller bowl, then serve.

SLICING ROOTS
When thinly slicing root vegetables, you should ideally use a mandoline. If you don't have one, a sharp small knife will do the job.

PER SERVING: 320 CALS | 16.4G FAT | 3.7G SAT FAT | 37.7G CARBS | 14.7G SUGARS | 8.4G FIBER | 7.8G PROTEIN | 1.8G SALT

FRUIT, NUT, AND SEED TRAIL MIX

This crunchy snack makes a wonderful alternative to commercial snacks for keeping hunger pangs at bay during the day.

MAKES: 2²/₃ CUPS (1 SERVING IS ABOUT 2 TABLESPOONS)
PREP: 10 MINS   COOK: 10 MINUTES

2 cups unblanched almonds
3 tablespoons pine nuts
2 tablespoons pumpkin seeds
3 tablespoons sunflower seeds
¼ cup dried banana chips
⅓ cup pitted and coarsely chopped dates
2 tablespoons oat bran
½ teaspoon ground allspice
1 medium egg white

1. Preheat the oven to 400°F. Put the almonds, pine nuts, pumpkin and sunflower seeds, banana chips, dates, oat bran, and allspice in a large bowl and mix well.

2. Lightly beat the egg white with a fork. Add to the nuts, stirring to coat all the ingredients evenly.

3. Spread the mixture out on a large baking sheet in a single layer. Bake for 8–10 minutes, or until crisp and lightly browned.

4. Let cool completely. Serve or pack into an airtight container and eat within five days.

ALSO TRY
For a savory mix, replace the bananas and dates with ²/₃ cup cashew nuts, and the allspice with 1 teaspoon of mild curry powder and a large pinch of sea salt.

PER SERVING: 75 CALS | 6G FAT | 0.5G SAT FAT | 2.5G CARBS | 1G SUGARS | 1G FIBER | 2.5G PROTEIN | TRACE SALT

TURKEY NUGGETS WITH RED CABBAGE AND KALE SLAW

Forget deep-fried chicken; this oven-baked, crispy-coated turkey version is quick and easy to make, and healthier.

SERVES: 4
PREP: 20 MINS COOK: 15 MINS

⅓ cup flaxseed
⅓ cup sesame seeds
2 eggs
1 pound skinless, boneless turkey breast, thinly sliced
3 tablespoons virgin olive oil
sea salt and pepper, to taste

RED CABBAGE AND KALE SLAW

1¼ cups thinly shredded red cabbage
⅓ cup thinly shredded kale
1 carrot, shredded
1 Golden Delicious, Red Delicious, Pink Lady, or other sweet, crisp apple, cored and coarsely grated
1 teaspoon caraway seeds
¼ cup Greek-style plain yogurt

1. Preheat the oven to 425°F and put a large baking sheet in it to preheat.

2. To make the slaw, put the red cabbage, kale, and carrot in a bowl and mix well. Add the apple, caraway seeds, and yogurt, season with salt and pepper to taste, and mix well. Cover and chill in the refrigerator until needed.

3. Put the flaxseed in a spice mill or blender and process until coarsely ground. Add the sesame seeds and process for a few seconds. Turn out the mixture onto a plate.

4. Crack the eggs into a shallow dish, season with salt and pepper, and beat lightly with a fork.

5. Dip each turkey slice into the eggs, then lift it out with a fork and dip both sides into the seed mixture to coat. Brush the hot baking sheet with a little oil, add the turkey slices in a single layer, then drizzle with a little extra oil.

6. Bake the turkey, turning the slices once and moving them from the corners into the center of the baking sheet, for 15 minutes, or until golden brown and cooked through. Cut one of the larger turkey nuggets in half to check that the meat is no longer pink. Any juices that run out should be clear and piping hot with steam rising. Serve the nuggets with the slaw.

MAKE IT LIGHTER

Put a little oil in a small pump-action plastic sprayer and use this to spray a fine oil mist over the turkey before baking.

PER SERVING: 471 CALS | 27G FAT | 4.2G SAT FAT | 21.3G CARBS | 8.6G SUGARS | 9.2G FIBER | 38.4G PROTEIN | 1.8G SALT

FISH BURGERS

These fish burgers can be made and shaped up to a day in advance and stored in the refrigerator, ready to bake 30 minutes before lunch.

SERVES: 4

PREP: 45 MINS   CHILL: 30 MINS   COOK: 50 MINS

4 russet potatoes, cut into chunks
1 pound boneless firm white fish fillets, such as Alaskan pollock, halibut, or cod
2 tablespoons unsalted butter
finely grated zest and juice of 1 unwaxed lemon
¼ cup milk
¼ cup finely chopped fresh flat-leaf parsley
1 cup finely snipped fresh chives
1 egg
4 slices of homemade whole wheat bread (see page 24), processed in a food processor to make crumbs
½ cup finely grated Parmesan cheese
1 tablespoon virgin olive oil
sea salt and pepper, to taste
3 cups mixed salad greens, to serve
lemon wedges, to serve

OLIVE TARTAR SAUCE
¾ cup pitted and chopped herb-marinated green and black ripe olives
⅔ cup plain yogurt

1. Fill the bottom of a steamer halfway with water, bring to a boil, then add the potatoes to the water and cook for 15 minutes. Put the fish in the steamer top in a single layer, cover with a lid, and steam for 8–10 minutes, or until it flakes easily when pressed with a knife and the potatoes are tender.

2. Drain the potatoes, add the butter, lemon zest and juice, and 2 tablespoons of milk, and mash together. Remove any skin from the fish, flake the flesh into bite-size pieces, then add it to the mash with ¼ oz each of the parsley and chives, and a little salt and pepper, and fold everything together carefully.

3. Divide the mixture into eight portions, then shape each into a thick patty and let cool.

4. Crack the egg into a shallow bowl, add the remaining 2 tablespoons of milk, and beat with a fork. Put the bread crumbs, remaining parsley, ¼ cup of the chives, and the Parmesan on a plate and mix together. Coat each fish burger in the egg, then dip it into the crumb mixture to coat completely. Chill in the refrigerator for 30 minutes.

5. Preheat the oven to 400°F. Brush a large baking sheet with a little oil, add the fish burgers, then drizzle with a little extra oil. Bake for 25–30 minutes, turning over halfway through cooking, until browned and piping hot.

6. To make the olive tartare sauce, put the olives, yogurt, remaining chives and a little salt and pepper in a bowl and mix well. Serve the fish burgers with spoonfuls of the sauce, the salad greens and lemon wedges for squeezing over the fish burgers.

BUYING FISH
When buying fish from your local supermarket or fish dealer, look out for the Marine Stewardship Council (MSC) approved logo.

PER SERVING: 400 CALS | 15.9G FAT | 7G SAT FAT | 33.2G CARBS | 5.1G SUGARS | 4.8G FIBER | 31.3G PROTEIN | 3.2G SALT

STUFFED EGGPLANTS

Enjoy this dish with a green salad and baby new potatoes for a sunshine lunch. Quinoa is processed to remove bitter compounds, but its nutrition levels are superhigh.

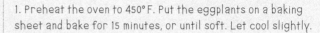

SERVES: 4

PREP: 30 MINS   COOK: 50 MINS

2 eggplants
1 tablespoon virgin olive oil
1 small onion, finely chopped
2 garlic cloves, finely chopped
¾ cup white quinoa
1½ cups homemade vegetable stock
(see page 16)
¼ cup unblanched almonds, thinly sliced
and toasted
2 tablespoons finely chopped fresh mint,
plus a few sprigs to garnish
3 ounces feta cheese, drained and crumbled
sea salt and pepper, to taste

1. Preheat the oven to 450°F. Put the eggplants on a baking sheet and bake for 15 minutes, or until soft. Let cool slightly.

2. Cut each eggplant in half lengthwise and scoop out the flesh, leaving a ¼-inch-thick border inside the skin so they hold their shape. Chop the flesh.

3. Heat the oil in a large, heavy skillet over medium-high heat. Add the onion and garlic and cook, stirring occasionally, for 5 minutes, or until soft. Add the quinoa, stock, eggplant flesh, 1 teaspoon of salt, and a pinch of pepper. Reduce the heat to medium-low, cover, and cook for 15 minutes, or until the quinoa is cooked through. Remove from the heat and stir in the almonds, mint, and half the feta.

4. Divide the quinoa mixture equally between the eggplant skins and top with the remaining feta. Bake for 10–15 minutes, or until the feta is bubbling and beginning to brown. Garnish with the mint sprigs and serve.

EGGPLANT FACTS
Eggplants are packed with antioxidants, many of the B vitamins, and minerals, such as manganese, copper, iodine, and potassium.

PER SERVING: 287 CALS | 14G FAT | 4.2G SAT FAT | 29G CARBS | 9G SUGARS | 9G FIBER | 12.5G PROTEIN | 2.1G SALT

TAGLIATELLE WITH ROASTED SQUASH AND WALNUT PESTO

Roasted butternut squash or pumpkin tastes great with homemade walnut pesto. Make extra pesto and keep it in the refrigerator for up to two days.

SERVES: 4
PREP: 20 MINS   COOK: 25 MINS

3 cups seeded and peeled ³/₄–inch
butternut squash or pumpkin slices
2 tablespoons virgin olive oil
1 pound fresh whole wheat tagliatelle
sea salt flakes and pepper, to taste

WALNUT PESTO
³/₄ cup walnut pieces
¹/₃ cup virgin olive oil
¹/₃ cup fresh basil
1 ounce Parmesan cheese, thinly shaved,
plus extra to serve
2¹/₂ cups arugula leaves

1. Preheat the oven to 400°F. Arrange the squash on a large baking sheet in a single layer. Drizzle with the oil and season with salt and pepper. Roast for 20–25 minutes, or until just tender.

2. Meanwhile, to make the pesto, put the walnuts in a large skillet and toast for 2–3 minutes, or until just beginning to brown. Transfer to a food processor or blender, pour in the oil, and process until coarsely ground. Add the basil, cheese, and half the arugula leaves and process again until you have a coarse pesto.

3. Bring a large saucepan of water to a boil, add the tagliatelle, and cook for 3–4 minutes, or according to the package directions, until al dente.

4. Drain the pasta, reserving a little of the cooking water. Return the pasta to the pan. Cut the squash into cubes and add them to the pasta. Drizzle with the pesto and gently toss together, adding a little of the reserved pasta water if needed to loosen the sauce. Top with the remaining arugula.

5. Spoon into bowls and serve with extra cheese.

MAKE IT LIGHTER
Toss the roasted squash and walnut pesto
with crisp salad greens instead of
pasta for a lighter meal.

PER SERVING: 808 CALS | 49.9G FAT | 8.2G SAT FAT | 74.7G CARBS | 4.5G SUGARS | 11.1G FIBER | 25.5G PROTEIN | 1.9G SALT

ROASTED BEET AND FARRO SALAD

Beets are low in fat, full of vitamins and minerals, packed with antioxidants, and delicious, especially when sharing a plate with earthy farro and walnuts.

SERVES: 4
PREP: 20 MINS   COOK: 40 MINS

2 raw beets, quartered
3 sprigs of fresh thyme
⅓ cup walnut oil
⅔ cup farro, rinsed
1 large red bell pepper, halved lengthwise and seeded
¼ cup coarsely chopped walnuts
3 cups arugula leaves
thick balsamic vinegar, for drizzling
sea salt and pepper, to taste

1. Preheat the oven to 375°F. Preheat the broiler to high. Cut out two squares of aluminum foil.

2. Divide the beets and thyme between the foil squares. Sprinkle with a little of the oil and season with salt and pepper. Wrap in a loose package, sealing the edges, and place on a baking sheet. Roast for 30–40 minutes, or until tender.

3. Meanwhile, put the farro in a saucepan, cover with water, and add ½ teaspoon of salt. Bring to a boil, then reduce the heat, cover, and simmer for 20 minutes, or according to the package directions, until the grains are tender. Drain the farro and transfer to a dish.

4. Meanwhile, put the red bell pepper halves, cut side down, on the broiler pan and broil for 10 minutes, or until blackened. Cover with a clean dish towel and let stand for 10 minutes. Remove and discard the skin and coarsely chop the flesh.

5. Divide the cooked farro between four plates. Slice the beet quarters in half, arrange on top of the farro and toss. Sprinkle with the red pepper, walnuts, and arugula.

6. Drizzle with the remaining oil and some balsamic vinegar. Serve immediately.

ALSO TRY
This salad works equally well with barley instead of farro. The barley will need boiling for 35 minutes.

PER SERVING: 315 CALS | 21.9G FAT | 2G SAT FAT | 25.6G CARBS | 7.6G SUGARS | 4.3G FIBER | 5.8G PROTEIN | 1.6G SALT

WHOLE WHEAT SPINACH, PEA, AND FETA TART

*Baked and unfilled tart crusts freeze well, so why not make two,
then fill and enjoy one now and wrap and freeze the second for another time?*

SERVES: 6
PREP: 30 MINS   CHILL: 30 MINS
COOK: 1 HOUR 10 MINS   COOL: 20 MINS

3 tablespoons unsalted butter
3 scallions, thinly sliced
7 cups baby spinach
²/₃ cup shelled peas
3 eggs
1 cup milk
3¹/₂ ounces feta cheese, drained and finely crumbled
8 cherry tomatoes
sea salt and pepper, to taste

PASTRY DOUGH
1 stick unsalted butter, cut into cubes
1³/₄ cups whole wheat flour, plus extra to dust
2 eggs, beaten

1. To make the dough, put the butter and flour in a mixing bowl and season with salt and pepper. Rub the butter into the flour until it resembles fine crumbs. Gradually mix in enough egg to make a soft but not sticky dough.

2. Lightly dust a work surface with whole wheat flour. Knead the dough gently, then roll it out on the work surface to a little larger than a 10-inch loose-bottom tart pan. Lift the dough over the rolling pin, ease it into the pan, and press it into the sides. Trim the dough so that it stands a little above the top of the pan to allow for shrinkage, then prick the bottom with a fork.

3. Cover the tart shell with plastic wrap and chill in the refrigerator for 15–30 minutes. Meanwhile, preheat the oven to 375°F.

4. To make the filling, melt the butter in a skillet over medium heat. Add the scallions and cook for 2–3 minutes, or until softened. Add the spinach, turn the heat to high, and cook, stirring, until wilted. Set aside to cool.

5. Cook the peas in a small saucepan of boiling water for 2 minutes. Drain, then plunge into iced water and drain again. Crack the eggs into a small bowl, add the milk, season with salt and pepper, and beat with a fork.

6. Line the tart shell with a large sheet of parchment paper, add pie weights or dried beans, and place on a baking sheet. Bake for 10 minutes, then remove the paper and weights and bake for an additional 5 minutes, or until the bottom of the tart is crisp and dry.

7. Drain any cooking juices from the scallions and spinach into the eggs. Put the scallion mixture in the tart crust, add the peas, then sprinkle with the cheese. Fork the eggs and milk together once again, then pour into the tart crust and dot the tomatoes over the top. Bake for 40–50 minutes, or until set and golden. Let cool for 20 minutes, then serve.

PASTRY TIPS
Whole wheat flour adds a wonderful nuttiness to pastry, but it can be difficult to handle. If it breaks when you line the tart pan, just press the cracks together or patch with some of the scraps and stick in place with any remaining egg or a little water.

PER SERVING: 458 CALS | 29.4G FAT | 16.9G SAT FAT | 34.9G CARBS | 4.8G SUGARS | 6G FIBER | 16.8G PROTEIN | 2.1G SALT

ROASTED MEDITERRANEAN VEGETABLE PIZZAS

Making your own pizzas might seem like a lot of work, but they are actually easy to put together and a great way to encourage children to cook.

SERVES: 4

PREP: 50 MINS   RISE: 1 HOUR   COOK: 30 MINS

8 plum tomatoes, halved
1 red onion, cut into 8 wedges
1 eggplant, halved and sliced
1 red and 1 orange bell pepper, quartered and seeded
2 small zucchini, sliced
3 tablespoons virgin olive oil, plus extra to serve
1/3 cup basil leaves, plus extra to garnish
2 teaspoons aged balsamic vinegar
6 ounces goat cheese, crumbled
sea salt flakes and pepper, to taste

PIZZA CRUSTS

2 cups whole wheat flour, plus extra to dust
1/2 teaspoon sea salt
1 teaspoon packed dark brown sugar
1 teaspoon active dry yeast
1 tablespoon virgin olive oil
2/3–3/4 cup warm water

FABULOUS FRESH YEAST

Active dry yeast makes a great pantry standby, but if you would prefer to use fresh yeast, try to buy it from your local baker. Crumble 2 teaspoons of fresh yeast and mix it with the sugar, then blend with half the warm water. Set aside for 15 minutes, or until the liquid begins to froth, then mix into the flour with the remaining ingredients. Keep any leftover yeast in paper in an airtight container in the refrigerator for no more than three days.

1. Preheat the oven to 425°F. To make the pizza crusts, put the flour, salt, sugar, and yeast in a mixing bowl and stir. Add the oil, then gradually mix in enough warm water to make a soft but not sticky dough.

2. Lightly dust a work surface with flour. Knead the dough on the surface for 5 minutes, until smooth and elastic. Return it to the bowl, cover with a clean dish towel, and put it in a warm place for 45 minutes, or until doubled in size.

3. Arrange the tomatoes and red onion on a baking sheet in a single layer. Arrange the eggplant and bell peppers, cut side down, on a second baking sheet in a single layer. Arrange the zucchini on a third baking sheet in a single layer. Drizzle with a little oil and sprinkle with salt and pepper. Roast for 15 minutes, then take out the zucchini. Roast the other vegetables for an additional 5 minutes. Wrap the bell peppers in aluminum foil and let cool, then cut into slices.

4. Remove and discard the tomato skins, if desired, then chop the tomatoes, onion, and basil and mix with the vinegar.

5. Lightly flour two baking sheets. Knead the dough, cut it into two pieces, and roll out each piece into an oval 12 inches long by 6 inches wide. Transfer them to the baking sheets, spoon the tomato mixture over them, then top with the roasted vegetables. Let rise for 15 minutes.

6. Sprinkle the goat cheese over the pizzas, then bake for 10 minutes, or until the crusts are cooked and the cheese has melted. Sprinkle with a little extra oil and basil. Cut each pizza into wedges and serve immediately.

PER SERVING: 595 CALS | 30.3G FAT | 11.2G SAT FAT | 66.1G CARBS | 13.2G SUGARS | 14.3G FIBER | 21.6G PROTEIN | 2.8G SALT

BEET FALAFEL WITH PITAS

Traditionally deep fried, these ruby-color falafels are flavored with cumin and sumac, then roasted in the oven. Serve in homemade pita bread with a cucumber-yogurt dip.

SERVES: 4
PREP: 1 HOUR   RISE: 55 MINS   COOK: 35 MINS

a little whole wheat all-purpose flour, to dust
1 quantity kneaded and risen pizza crust dough (see page 70) made with 1 teaspoon coarsely crushed cumin seeds added with the yeast
2 (15-ounce) cans of chickpeas in water, drained
1 red onion, finely chopped
2 garlic cloves, thinly sliced
1 teaspoon cumin seeds, coarsely crushed
1 teaspoon sumac seeds
1 teaspoon baking powder
2 raw beets, coarsely grated
3 tablespoons virgin olive oil, to brush
sea salt and pepper
shredded lettuce, to serve

CUCUMBER-YOGURT DIP
½ cucumber, halved, seeded and finely chopped
⅔ cup plain yogurt
2 tablespoons finely chopped fresh mint

1. Preheat the oven to 425°F. To make the pita bread, lightly dust a work surface with flour. Knead the dough gently, then cut it into four pieces and roll out each piece on the work surface into an oval about the size of your hand. Let rise for 10 minutes.

2. Lightly flour two baking sheets, then put them in the oven for 5 minutes. Add the breads to the hot baking sheets and bake for 5–10 minutes, or until puffed and lightly browned. Wrap them in a clean dish towel to keep them soft.

3. Meanwhile, put the chickpeas in a food processor or blender, in small batches, and process into a coarse paste, scraping down the sides of the bowl several times with a spatula. Transfer to a bowl. Add the red onion, garlic, cumin, sumac, baking powder, and beets, season well with salt and pepper, then mix together with a fork.

4. Spoon the mixture into 20 mounds on a cutting board, then squeeze them into balls. Brush a large roasting pan with a little oil, then put it in the oven for 5 minutes. Add the falafels and brush generously with more oil. Roast for 20–25 minutes, turning once or twice, until browned and the chickpeas and beets are cooked through; break one open and taste to check.

5. Meanwhile, to make the cucumber-yogurt dip, put the cucumber, yogurt, and mint in a bowl, season with salt and pepper, and mix well.

6. To serve, split the warm pita breads open, spoon in the shredded lettuce, cucumber-yogurt dip, and five falafels per pita, and serve.

FREEZING PITA BREAD
Make a double quantity of pita bread and freeze half the cooked breads in a sealed plastic bag. Defrost at room temperature for 1 hour, then warm in a skillet for 2 minutes on each side.

PER SERVING: 638 CALS | 21.8G FAT | 3.5G SAT FAT | 93.4G CARBS | 14.1G SUGARS | 19.9G FIBER | 23.3G PROTEIN | 2.5G SALT

MAIN DISHES

SPICY HAMBURGERS
WITH GUACAMOLE AND WEDGES

A good hamburger is hard to beat, and if you make your own,
you'll know what is in it and where the meat has come from.
Grind the steak in a food processor or meat grinder.

SERVES: 4

PREP: 1 HOUR   RISE: 1½ HOURS   COOK: 1 HOUR

1 pound sirloin steak, visible fat removed, diced
½ teaspoon chili powder
2 teaspoons cumin seeds, coarsely crushed
1 tablespoon fresh thyme leaves
5 russet potatoes, unpeeled,
scrubbed and cut into wedges
3 tablespoons virgin olive oil
1 teaspoon paprika
sea salt and pepper, to taste

GUACAMOLE
1 large avocado, pitted and peeled
juice of 1 lime
2 scallions, finely chopped

TO SERVE
4 spelt breakfast rolls (see page 38, but shape 10 rolls
instead of 16, let rise for 45 minutes instead of
overnight, and bake for 15–18 minutes), halved
1 romaine lettuce heart, shredded
handful of arugula leaves
2 large tomatoes, sliced

1. Preheat the oven to 400°F. With the motor running on a food processor, drop in a few pieces of steak at a time, until it has all been coarsely chopped. Alternatively, press the pieces through a manual meat grinder on the coarse setting.

2. Put the chili powder, half the cumin seeds, half the thyme, and a little salt and pepper into a bowl and mix well. Rub it into the steak, then shape the mixture into four patties. Cover and chill in the refrigerator for 15 minutes.

3. Meanwhile, bring a saucepan of water to a boil, add the potato wedges, and cook for 4–5 minutes, or until almost tender. Drain well and transfer to a roasting pan. Drizzle the wedges with 2 tablespoons of oil, then turn them several times until they are well coated. Sprinkle with the paprika, remaining cumin and thyme, and a little salt and pepper. Bake, turning once, for 25–30 minutes, or until golden brown.

4. For the guacamole, put the avocado in a shallow bowl and mash with a fork. Add the lime juice and scallions, season with a little salt and pepper, and mix well.

5. Preheat the broiler to medium–high. Brush the patties with a little of the remaining oil, then cook, turning halfway through, for 8–10 minutes, or a little less for those who prefer their burgers pink in the middle. Let stand for a few minutes. Meanwhile, toast the rolls, then top the bottom half of the rolls with lettuce, arugula, and tomatoes, the hot burgers, and a spoonful of guacamole before finishing with the lids. Serve with the potato wedges.

AVOCADO TIP
Avocado flesh quickly turns brown, even when mixed with lime juice, so don't be tempted to peel and mash the flesh for the guacamole until you are ready to cook the burgers.

PER SERVING: 695 CALS | 28.9G FAT | 5.8G SAT FAT | 63.4G CARBS | 9.9G SUGARS | 13.8G FIBER | 49.1G PROTEIN | 1.4G SALT

YAM AND BEEF STEW
WITH WHOLE-GRAIN COUSCOUS

Your kitchen will be filled with delicious smells as this warming and nutritious dish slowly simmers in your oven, leaving you to get on with something else.

SERVES: 4

PREP: 30 MINS   CHILL: OVERNIGHT   COOK: 1½ HOURS

1¾ pounds boneless beef chuck,
cut into 1-inch cubes
2 onions, coarsely chopped
1⅓ cups cubed yams
7 ounces baby new potatoes, unpeeled, scrubbed
and halved
1 (15-ounce) can chickpeas in water,
drained and rinsed
1 (14½-ounce) can diced tomatoes
1 cup water
sea salt and pepper, to taste

MARINADE
2 tablespoons virgin olive oil
2 tablespoons finely chopped fresh cilantro
2 cinnamon sticks
1 tablespoon runny honey
1 teaspoon paprika
1 teaspoon ground cumin
1 teaspoon harissa paste

COUSCOUS
1 cup whole-grain couscous
1 tablespoon coarsely chopped fresh flat-leaf parsley
6 scallions, thinly sliced
juice of 1 lemon
2 tablespoons virgin olive oil

1. Put the beef in a large bowl. Add the marinade ingredients and 1 teaspoon of salt and stir well. Cover and chill in the refrigerator for 6 hours or overnight.

2. Preheat the oven to 375°F. Transfer the meat and marinade to a casserole dish and add the onions, yams, potatoes, and chickpeas. Pour in the tomatoes and water and stir well. Bake for 1 hour.

3. Stir well and check the seasoning. If most of the liquid has been absorbed, add enough water to create a generous sauce. Bake for an additional 30 minutes, or until the meat is cooked and tender.

4. Meanwhile, fill a saucepan halfway with water and bring to a boil. Add the couscous and cook according to the package directions, or until just tender. Transfer to a strainer and drain well. Tip into a bowl, stir in the parsley and scallions, then drizzle with the lemon juice and oil.

5. Remove the cinnamon sticks from the stew and serve with the couscous.

PER SERVING: 836 CALS | 29.2G FAT | 7.3G SAT FAT | 88G CARBS | 12.6G SUGARS | 13.3G FIBER | 57.4G PROTEIN | 2.9G SALT

ROASTED PORK WITH ROSEMARY POTATOES

A traditional pairing, this simple roast is even more delicious when made with free-range pork and homegrown potatoes.

SERVES: 6
PREP: 15 MINS   COOK: 1 HOUR   REST: 20 MINS

2¼ pounds leg of pork
¼ cup virgin olive oil
sea salt

ROSEMARY POTATOES
5 russet potatoes, cut into chunks
4 sprigs of fresh rosemary, coarsely chopped

1. Preheat the oven to 425°F. Make sure that the skin of the pork is well scored and dry. Brush it with 1 tablespoon of oil and rub it with salt. Roast for 20 minutes, or until it has started to blister and is crisp.

2. Reduce the oven temperature to 400°F. Roast the pork for an additional 40 minutes, or until it is cooked through and the skin is crisp and golden. Pierce the thickest part of the leg with the tip of a sharp knife; any juices should be piping hot with no sign of red or pink. Let rest for 20 minutes before carving into slices.

3. Meanwhile, for the rosemary potatoes, bring a saucepan of water to a boil, add the potatoes and rosemary, toss, and cook for 4–5 minutes. Drain well and transfer to a roasting pan. Drizzle with the remaining oil, then turn the potatoes several times until they are well coated. Roast, turning once, for 40 minutes, or until golden brown.

4. Transfer the pork and potatoes to a serving plate and sprinkle the potatoes with a little salt. Serve immediately with the pork.

ROAST POTATOES
Choose potatoes with a mealy texture, such as russets, for roasting, to achieve a nice, crispy result. Firm, waxy potatoes won't roast as well.

PER SERVING: 674 CALS | 39.7G FAT | 11G SAT FAT | 26G CARBS | 1.9G SUGARS | 4G FIBER | 51G PROTEIN | 2.3G SALT

SPICED TURKEY STEW WITH WHOLE-GRAIN COUSCOUS

Capture the flavors of Middle Eastern cooking with this easy, lightly spiced stove-top turkey stew.

SERVES: 4
PREP: 20 MINS   COOK: 25 MINS

1 tablespoon virgin olive oil
1 pound skinless, boneless turkey breast, cut into ¾-inch pieces
1 onion, coarsely chopped
2 garlic cloves, finely chopped
1 red and 1 orange bell pepper, seeded and coarsely chopped
4 tomatoes, coarsely chopped
1 teaspoon cumin seeds, coarsely crushed
1 teaspoon paprika
finely grated zest and juice of 1 unwaxed lemon
sea salt and pepper, to taste

TO SERVE

1 cup whole-grain giant couscous
2 tablespoons coarsely chopped fresh flat-leaf parsley
2 tablespoons coarsely chopped fresh cilantro

1. Heat the oil in a large skillet over medium heat. Add the turkey, a few pieces at a time, then add the onion. Sauté, stirring, for 5 minutes, or until the turkey is golden.

2. Add the garlic, red and orange bell peppers, and tomatoes, then stir in the cumin seeds and paprika. Add the lemon juice and season with salt and pepper. Stir well, then cover and cook, stirring from time to time, for 20 minutes, or until the tomatoes have formed a thick sauce and the turkey is cooked through and the juices run clear with no sign of pink when a piece is cut in half.

3. Meanwhile, fill a saucepan halfway with water and bring to a boil. Add the couscous and cook according to the package directions, or until just tender. Transfer to a strainer and drain well.

4. Spoon the couscous onto plates and top with the turkey stew. Mix the parsley and cilantro with the lemon zest, then sprinkle the mixture over the stew and serve.

GOOD TURKEY
Turkey makes a great low-fat, quick-cook dinner, especially without the skin.

PER SERVING: 399 CALS | 6.6G FAT | 1.3G SAT FAT | 36G CARBS | 8.1G SUGARS | 7.2G FIBER | 37.5G PROTEIN | 0.9G SALT

CHICKEN WITH POMEGRANATE AND BEET TABBOULEH

This version of tabbouleh is made with whole-grain wheat berries.
High in fiber, it is a great alternative to rice or pasta.

SERVES: 4
PREP: 25 MINS   COOK: 25 MINS

1⅓ cups wheat berries
4 raw beets, cut into cubes
1 pound skinless, boneless chicken
breasts, thinly sliced
1 small red onion, thinly sliced
12 cherry tomatoes, halved
seeds of 1 small pomegranate
2 tablespoons coarsely chopped fresh mint
2½ cups baby spinach
sea salt and pepper, to taste

DRESSING
juice of 1 lemon
¼ cup virgin olive oil
2 garlic cloves, finely chopped
1 teaspoon packed light brown sugar

1. Fill the bottom of a steamer with water, bring to a boil, then add the wheat berries to the water. Put the beets in the steamer top, cover with a lid, and steam for 20–25 minutes, or until the wheat berries and beets are cooked. Drain the wheat berries.

2. Meanwhile, to make the dressing, put the lemon juice, oil, garlic, and sugar in a screw-lid jar, season with salt and pepper, then screw on the lid and shake well.

3. Put the chicken in a bowl, add half the dressing, and toss well. Preheat a ridged broiler pan over medium-high heat. Add the chicken and cook, turning once or twice, for 8–10 minutes, or until golden and cooked through. Cut one of the larger slices of chicken in half to check that the meat is no longer pink. Any juices that run out should be clear and piping hot with steam rising.

4. Put the red onion, tomatoes, and pomegranate seeds in a large shallow bowl. Add the wheat berries, beets and mint. Divide the spinach among four plates, spoon the wheat berry mixture over them, then arrange the chicken on top. Serve with the remaining dressing in a small pitcher.

LOVE LEFTOVERS
Leftovers can be packed in plastic containers and stored in the refrigerator—but keep the dressing separate so that the salad doesn't go limp.

PER SERVING: 545 CALS | 17.2G FAT | 2G SAT FAT | 62.2G CARBS | 15G SUGARS | 12.3G FIBER | 39.4G PROTEIN | 1.1G SALT

CHEDDAR AND APPLE-STUFFED CHICKEN BREASTS

A new and tasty spin on chicken Kiev, this simple and delicious dish is sure to be a hit with the family.

SERVES: 4

PREP: 30 MINS   COOK: 35 MINS

4 thick skinless, boneless chicken breasts
1 tablespoon virgin olive oil, plus extra to grease
1 small onion, finely chopped
1 celery stalk, finely chopped
1/4 teaspoon dried sage
1 Pippin or other crisp apple, cored and diced
3/4 cup shredded cheddar cheese
2 tablespoons finely chopped fresh flat-leaf parsley
6 slices of prosciutto, visible fat removed
sea salt and pepper, to taste
5 1/2 ounces baby broccoli, to serve
1 cup shelled peas, to serve

1. Preheat the oven to 375°F. Lightly oil a small roasting pan.

2. Put a chicken breast on a cutting board, rounded side up. Use a small, sharp knife to cut a pocket along the length of the chicken breast, cutting as deep as you can without cutting through to the other side or the ends. Repeat with the remaining breasts, then cover and transfer to the refrigerator.

3. To make the stuffing, heat 2 teaspoons of oil in a skillet over medium heat. Add the onion, celery, and sage and sauté, stirring, for 3–5 minutes, or until soft. Stir in the apple and cook for 2 minutes, or until soft but not falling apart. Stir in the cheese and parsley and season with salt and pepper.

4. Divide the stuffing among the chicken pockets. Wrap one and a half slices of ham around each breast, then rub the tops with the remaining oil.

5. Transfer the chicken to the prepared pan and roast for 20–25 minutes, or until the chicken is cooked through and the juices are piping hot with steam rising and run clear with no sign of pink when the tip of a sharp knife is inserted into the thickest part of the meat.

6. Cover with aluminum foil and let stand for 3–5 minutes. Bring a saucepan of water to a boil, add the broccoli and peas, and cook for 3–4 minutes, then drain well. Serve the chicken with the green vegetables.

PER SERVING: 329 CALS | 17G FAT | 6.8G SAT FAT | 8G CARBS | 5.2G SUGARS | 1.5G FIBER | 35G PROTEIN | 2.1G SALT

SEARED WILD SALMON WITH GARDEN GREENS

Quick and easy to prepare, this light and summery dinner makes the best of the early beans and asparagus.

SERVES: 4
PREP: 20 MINS   COOK: 15 MINS

1 pound baby new potatoes, unpeeled, scrubbed, and any larger ones halved
1 tablespoon virgin olive oil
finely grated zest and juice of 1 unwaxed lemon
1 teaspoon set honey
1 teaspoon whole-grain mustard
4 wild salmon steaks, 5½ ounces each
2½ cups thinly sliced green beans
16 asparagus spears
3 cups sugar snap peas
1 fennel bulb, thinly sliced, green feathery tops torn into pieces
⅓ cup crème fraîche or plain Greek-style yogurt
sea salt and pepper

1. Fill the bottom of a steamer halfway with water, bring to a boil, then add the potatoes to the water and cook for 15 minutes.

2. Preheat the broiler to medium-high and line the broiler pan with aluminum foil. Mix the oil, lemon zest and juice, honey, and mustard together in a small bowl, then stir in a little salt and pepper. Arrange the salmon on the broiler pan, spoon the lemon mixture over the fish, and broil, turning once, for 8–10 minutes, or until browned and the fish flakes easily when pressed with a knife.

3. Put the beans in the steamer, set over the potatoes, cover with a lid, and steam for the last 6 minutes. Add the asparagus and sugar snap peas 3 minutes before the end of the cooking time. Add the sliced fennel 1 minute before the end of the cooking time.

4. Drain the potatoes, season with salt and pepper, and coarsely crush with a fork. Spoon into the center of four plates. Mix the green vegetables with the crème fraîche and fennel tops, then spoon them over the potatoes. Remove the skin from the salmon, then lay it on top of the vegetables and spoon the lemony pan juices over the fish. Serve immediately.

BUYING SALMON
Salmon farming has quadrupled in the last 20 years, so check the label carefully to make sure it is wild, and don't be afraid to ask the assistant where it was caught.

PER SERVING: 528 CALS | 27.7G FAT | 7.2G SAT FAT | 32.9G CARBS | 9.1G SUGARS | 7.9G FIBER | 37.3G PROTEIN | 1.1G SALT

BUTTER-FRIED SOLE

Look for sustainable fish caught the day you plan to eat it
—the flavor will be much better. Frozen fish is also
recommended because it's often caught and frozen on the same day.

SERVES: 2
PREP: 20 MINS   COOK: 12 MINS

½ cup milk
⅓ cup brown rice flour
4 sole fillets, 6 ounces each, skinned
16 asparagus spears
6 tablespoons unsalted butter
juice of ½ lemon, plus 1 lemon, cut into wedges, to serve
sea salt and pepper, to taste
2 tablespoons coarsely chopped fresh flat-leaf parsley, to garnish

1. Pour the milk into a shallow bowl at least as large as each fillet and put the flour on a plate. Season each fillet on both sides with salt and pepper.

2. Bring a saucepan of water to a boil, add the asparagus, and cook for 3–5 minutes, then drain well and keep warm.

3. Working with one sole fillet at a time, pull it quickly through the milk, then dip it in the flour, turn once to coat all over, and shake off any excess flour. Transfer it to a plate and continue until all the fillets are prepared.

4. Melt half the butter in a skillet large enough to hold the fillets in a single layer over medium-high heat. Add the fillets, skinned side down, and cook for 2 minutes.

5. Turn over the fillets and cook for 2–3 minutes, or until the flesh flakes easily. Transfer to two plates, skinned side up, and set aside.

6. Reduce the heat to medium and melt the remaining butter in the pan. When it stops foaming, add the lemon juice and stir, scraping the sediment from the bottom of the pan. Spoon the butter mixture over the fish and garnish with parsley. Serve with the asparagus and lemon wedges.

BUYING ASPARAGUS
To check for freshness, bend the bottom of the asparagus—you should only be able to bend the end of it.

PER SERVING: 753 CALS | 44.1G FAT | 24.5G SAT FAT | 39G CARBS | 6.2G SUGARS | 7.7G FIBER | 52.7G PROTEIN | 4.9G SALT

BAKED PARSNIPS AND TOMATOES

Serve this dish with salad and homemade whole wheat bread (see page 24) as a vegetarian dinner, or as a side dish with roasted meat.

SERVES: 4
PREP: 30 MINS   COOK: 50 MINS

3 tablespoons virgin olive oil
5 parsnips, thinly sliced lengthwise
1 teaspoon fresh thyme leaves
1¼ cups heavy cream
5 tomatoes, thinly sliced
1 teaspoon dried oregano
1⅓ cups shredded cheddar cheese
sea salt and pepper, to taste

1. Preheat the oven to 350°F. Heat the oil in a skillet over medium heat. Add the parsnips and thyme and season with salt and pepper. Cook, stirring often, for 6–8 minutes, or until softened. Do this in batches if necessary.

2. Spread half the parsnips over the bottom of a gratin dish. Pour over half the cream, then arrange half the tomatoes in an even layer on top. Season with salt and pepper and sprinkle over half the oregano and half the cheddar cheese. Top with the remaining parsnips and tomatoes. Sprinkle with the remaining oregano, season with salt and pepper, and pour the remaining cream over the vegetables. Sprinkle with the last of the cheddar cheese.

3. Cover with aluminum foil and bake for 40 minutes, or until the parsnips are tender. Remove the foil and return to the oven for 5–10 minutes, or until the top is golden and bubbling. Serve immediately.

ALSO TRY
Use Parmesan cheese instead of cheddar, or mozzarella for a pizza-style stringy texture.

PER SERVING: 639 CALS | 51G FAT | 26.7G SAT FAT | 35.4G CARBS | 11.4G SUGARS | 9.1G FIBER | 13.9G PROTEIN | 1.4G SALT

QUINOA WITH ROASTED VEGETABLES

Quinoa is an excellent source of protein, especially for vegetarians, because it contains all nine essential amino acids, which is unsusal for a plant.

SERVES: 2
PREP: 20 MINS   COOK: 30 MINS

1 red and 1 yellow bell pepper, seeded and
coarsely chopped
1 large zucchini, coarsely chopped
1 small fennel bulb, trimmed and cut into thin wedges
1 tablespoon virgin olive oil
2 teaspoons finely chopped fresh rosemary leaves
1 teaspoon finely chopped fresh thyme leaves
½ cup white quinoa, rinsed
1½ cups homemade vegetable stock
(see page 16)
2 garlic cloves, crushed
3 tablespoons finely chopped fresh flat-leaf parsley
⅓ cup pine nuts, toasted
sea salt and pepper, to taste

1. Preheat the oven to 425°F. Arrange the bell peppers, zucchini, and fennel in a large roasting pan in a single layer. Drizzle the oil over the vegetables and sprinkle with the rosemary and thyme. Season with salt and pepper and mix well. Roast for 25–30 minutes, or until tender and lightly charred.

2. Meanwhile, put the quinoa in a saucepan. Add the stock and garlic, bring to a boil, then cover and simmer over low heat for 10 minutes. Remove from the heat, but keep the pan covered for an additional 7 minutes to let the grains swell. Fluff up with a fork.

3. Transfer the quinoa to the roasting pan. Add the parsley and pine nuts and toss well. Serve warm or cold.

ALSO TRY
Use long-grain brown rice instead of quinoa;
brown rice takes 30–45 minutes to cook.

PER SERVING: 471 CALS | 25.3G FAT | 3.1G SAT FAT | 50.6G CARBS | 10.2G SUGARS | 9.7G FIBER | 13.3G PROTEIN | 3.2G SALT

VEGETABLE COCIDO

Quick and easy to make, this comforting Spanish-inspired stew is flavored with smoked paprika for a wonderful, deep spicy flavor.

SERVES: 4
PREP: 20 MINS   COOK: 50 MINS

2 tablespoons virgin olive oil
1 onion, coarsely chopped
1 eggplant, coarsely chopped
½ teaspoon smoked hot paprika
2 garlic cloves, finely chopped
1 large red bell pepper, seeded and coarsely chopped
9 ounces baby new potatoes, unpeeled and any larger ones halved
8 plum tomatoes, skinned and coarsely chopped
1 (15-ounce) can navy beans in water, drained
⅔ cup homemade vegetable stock (see page 16)
2 sprigs of fresh rosemary
2 zucchini, coarsely chopped
sea salt and pepper, to taste

1. Preheat the oven to 400°F. Heat 1 tablespoon of oil in a saucepan over medium heat. Add the onion and sauté for 5 minutes, or until softened. Add another tablespoon of oil, then add the eggplant, and sauté, stirring, for 5 minutes, or until just beginning to soften and brown.

2. Stir in the smoked paprika and garlic, then the red bell pepper, potatoes, and tomatoes. Add the navy beans, stock, and rosemary, then season with salt and pepper. Bring to a boil, cover, turn the heat down to medium-low, and simmer for 30 minutes, stirring from time to time.

3. Stir the zucchini into the stew, then cook, uncovered, for 10 minutes, or until all the vegetables are tender and the sauce has reduced slightly.

4. Ladle the stew into shallow bowls, discard the rosemary sprigs and serve.

SMOKED PAPRIKA
If you haven't used smoked hot paprika before, check before buying because it comes in two heat strengths: hot with the strength of chili powder or mild. Either one adds a great smoky flavor to this stew.

PER SERVING: 525 CALS | 26.1G FAT | 12.6G SAT FAT | 62.3G CARBS | 14.8G SUGARS | 18.5G FIBER | 14.6G PROTEIN | 1.8G SALT

SQUASH, KALE, AND FARRO STEW

This one-dish meal is supereasy to make and chockablock with nutrient-rich vegetables, grains, and beans.

SERVES: 6
PREP: 30 MINS   COOK: 55 MINS

2 tablespoons virgin olive oil
1 onion, finely chopped
2 teaspoons dried oregano
2 garlic cloves, thinly sliced
1 dense–fleshed squash (about 2¾ pounds), such as Kabocha or Crown Prince, peeled, seeded, and flesh cut into large cubes
1 (14½–ounce) can diced tomatoes
3 cups homemade vegetable stock (see page 16)
¾ cup quick–cook farro, rinsed
4 cups thickly shredded kale
1 (15–ounce) can chickpeas in water, drained and rinsed
1 cup coarsely chopped fresh cilantro
juice of 1 lime
sea salt and pepper, to taste

1. Heat the oil in a flameproof casserole dish or heavy saucepan over medium heat. Add the onion and sauté for 5 minutes, or until soft. Add the oregano and garlic and sauté for 2 minutes.

2. Add the squash and cook, covered, for 10 minutes. Add the tomatoes, stock, and farro, cover, and bring to a boil. Reduce the heat to medium–low and gently simmer for 20 minutes, stirring occasionally.

3. Add the kale and chickpeas and cook for an additional 15 minutes, or until all the vegetables and farro are tender.

4. Season with salt and pepper, and stir in the cilantro and lime juice just before serving.

QUICK-TO-COOK FARRO

Look for a quick-cooking farro (available online and in gourmet stores), so you can add it straight to the casserole without lengthy soaking or precooking. It may seem as if there is too much stock, but once you add the farro, most of it will be absorbed.

PER SERVING: 302 CALS | 7.7G FAT | 1.4G SAT FAT | 52.4G CARBS | 9.16G SUGARS | 8.9G FIBER | 10.4G PROTEIN | 2.4G SALT

DESSERTS AND BAKING

CELEBRATION CHOCOLATE CAKE

No one would guess from the appearance of this indulgent-looking cake that it is made with cooked beets for natural sweetness and whole wheat and brown rice flours.

SERVES 8

PREP: 40 MINS   COOK: 1 HOUR 20 MINS   COOL: 15 MINS

2½ raw beets, cut into cubes
5½ ounces semisweet chocolate, broken into pieces
¼ cup unsweetened cocoa powder
2 teaspoons baking powder
1 cup whole wheat flour
⅓ cup brown rice flour
1¾ sticks unsalted butter, softened and diced, plus extra to grease
1 cup plus 2 tablespoons firmly packed light brown sugar
4 eggs
2 tablespoons milk
1¼ cups heavy cream

1. Preheat the oven to 325°F. Lightly butter an 8-inch diameter round nonstick springform cake pan and line the bottom with a circle of parchment paper.

2. Fill the bottom of a steamer halfway with water, bring to a boil, then put the beets in the steamer top, cover with a lid, and steam for 15 minutes, or until tender. Transfer to a food processor and add ¼ cup of water from the bottom of the steamer. Puree until smooth, then let cool.

3. Put 4 ounces of the chocolate in a heatproof bowl set over a saucepan of gently simmering water, making sure the bowl doesn't touch the water. Let heat for 5 minutes, or until the chocolate has melted.

4. Sift the cocoa into a second bowl, then stir in the baking powder and whole wheat and rice flours.

5. Cream the butter and 1 cup of the sugar together in a large bowl. Beat in the eggs, one by one, adding spoonfuls of the flour mixture between each egg and beating well after each addition. Stir in the remaining flour mixture, the pureed beet, and melted chocolate, and beat until smooth, then mix in enough of the milk to make a soft dropping consistency.

6. Spoon the batter into the prepared pan and spread it into an even layer. Bake for 1 hour, or until well risen, the top is slightly cracked, and a toothpick comes out cleanly when inserted into the center of the cake. Let cool for 15 minutes, then remove from the pan, peel off the parchment paper, and transfer the cake to a wire rack.

7. To finish, melt the remaining chocolate in a heatproof bowl set over a saucepan of gently simmering water, making sure the bowl doesn't touch the water. Put the cream in a separate bowl, add the remaining 2 tablespoons of sugar, and beat until soft swirls form. Cut the cake in half and put the bottom half on a serving plate. Spoon one-third of the cream mixture onto the bottom of the cake, add the top half of the cake, then spoon the remaining cream on top. Drizzle with the melted chocolate. Cut into eight wedges to serve.

DARK CHOCOLATE
Studies show that eating a little dark chocolate every day can help lower your blood pressure.

PER SERVING: 662 CALS | 46.2G FAT | 27.5G SAT FAT | 57G CARBS | 33.7G SUGARS | 5.7G FIBER | 9.5G PROTEIN | 1G SALT

RAW CHOCOLATE ICE CREAM

No one will guess that this supersimple ice cream actually contains no chocolate, but instead it is packed with healthy bananas and cocoa powder.

SERVES: 4

PREP: 10 MINS   FREEZE: 3 HOURS

3 bananas, peeled
3 tablespoons unsweetened cocoa powder
1 tablespoon agave nectar

1. Cut the bananas into ¾-inch pieces. Place them in a freezer bag and freeze for 3 hours.

2. Put the frozen bananas in a food processor or blender. Add the cocoa powder and agave nectar and process until smooth. Scoop and serve immediately or refreeze for a firmer consistency.

BANANA BONUS
Bananas are high-energy fruit that are particularly loaded with fiber and potassium. They are considered to be effective in lowering blood pressure.

PER SERVING: 92 CALS | 0.8G FAT | 0.4G SAT FAT | 23.2G CARBS | 12.8G SUGARS | 3.3G FIBER | 1.6G PROTEIN | TRACE SALT

WHOLE-GRAIN CHOCOLATE BROWNIES

Who can resist a squishy, just-warm chocolate brownie? This version has about half the butter and sugar of traditional brownies, but still has a deep, rich chocolaty flavor.

MAKES: 20 BROWNIES
PREP: 20 MINS   COOK: 25 MINS   COOL: 15 MINS

1¼ cups pitted and chopped dates
½ cup water
3½ ounces semisweet chocolate, broken into pieces
5 tablespoons unsalted butter
¼ cup light brown sugar
¼ cup unsweetened cocoa powder
3 tablespoons whole wheat flour
1 teaspoon baking powder
2 eggs, beaten

1. Preheat the oven to 350°F. Line an 8-inch shallow square nonstick cake pan with a large square of parchment paper, snipping into the corners diagonally, then pressing the paper into the pan so that both the bottom and sides are lined.

2. Put the dates and water in a saucepan. Bring the water to a boil, cover, turn the heat down to medium–low, and simmer for 5 minutes, or until the dates have softened. Add the chocolate, butter, and sugar and stir until melted. Remove the pan from the heat.

3. Sift the cocoa into a bowl, then mix in the flour and baking powder. Add the eggs and the flour mixture to the saucepan and stir until smooth. Pour the batter into the prepared pan and spread it into an even layer. Bake for 18–20 minutes, or until well risen and the center is only just set.

4. Let cool in the pan for 15 minutes. Lift the cake out of the pan, cut it into 20 brownies, and peel off the paper.

ALSO TRY
Nut fans might want to toast ½ cup unblanched hazelnuts in a dry saucepan, coarsely chop them, and stir half into the brownie batter, then sprinkle the rest over the top just before baking.

PER BROWNIE: 91.6 CALS | 5.7G FAT | 3.4G SAT FAT | 9.4G CARBS | 6.7G SUGARS | 1.2G FIBER | 1.7G PROTEIN | 0.2G SALT

APPLESAUCE SPICED CUPCAKES

*These lemony apple cupcakes are satisfying and wholesome,
containing brown sugar and whole wheat flour.*

MAKES: 12 CUPCAKES
PREP: 40 MINS   COOK: 1 HOUR 15 MINS   COOL: 30 MINS

3 Rome, Pippin, or other sweet, crisp apples
finely grated zest and juice of 1 unwaxed lemon
2/3 cup whole wheat flour
1/2 cup brown rice flour
2 teaspoons baking powder
1/2 teaspoon ground allspice, plus extra to decorate
1 stick unsalted butter, softened and diced
1/2 cup firmly packed light brown sugar
2 eggs, beaten
1 cup crème fraîche or plain Greek-style yogurt

1. To make the applesauce, peel, core, and coarsely chop two of the apples, then put them in a saucepan. Add the lemon zest and half the juice, cover, and cook over medium–low heat for 5–10 minutes, or until soft. Mash until smooth, then let cool. Preheat the oven to 350°F.

2. Put 12 paper liners or squares of parchment paper in a 12–section muffin pan. Put the whole wheat and rice flours, baking powder, and allspice into a bowl and mix well.

3. Cream the butter and sugar together in a large bowl. Beat in alternate spoonfuls of the eggs and the flour mixture until it is all used, then stir in 2/3 cup applesauce (reserve any remaining for another time).

4. Spoon the batter into the paper liners. Bake for 15–18 minutes, or until well risen and the tops spring back when pressed with a fingertip. Let cool for 5 minutes, then transfer to a wire rack.

5. Line a baking sheet with parchment paper. Put the rest of the lemon juice in a medium bowl. Thinly slice the remaining apple, toss it in the lemon juice, then arrange it on the prepared baking sheet. Reduce the oven temperature to 225°F and cook the apple slices, turning once, for 30–45 minutes, or until just beginning to brown. Turn off the oven and let the apples cool inside it. Lift off the slices with a spatula and cut them in half.

6. Top each cupcake with a spoonful of crème fraîche or yogurt, sprinkle with allspice and put two apple slices on top.

MAKE IT SIMPLE
These cakes are great without any
decoration, and make a healthy addition
to the kids' school lunch bags.

PER CAKE: 224 CALS | 12.8G FAT | 7.5G SAT FAT | 25.6G CARBS | 13.9G SUGARS | 1.9G FIBER | 3.2G PROTEIN | 0.6G SALT

WHOLE WHEAT MUFFINS

These sweet, flavor-packed muffins are crammed with healthy ingredients, so you can enjoy them with none of the guilt you might feel if eating an ordinary muffin.

MAKES: 10 MUFFINS
PREP: 15 MINS COOK: 30 MINS

1³/₄ cups whole wheat flour
2 teaspoons baking powder
2 tablespoons packed light brown sugar
³/₄ cup finely chopped dried apricots
1 banana, peeled
1 tablespoon freshly squeezed orange juice
1 teaspoon finely grated orange zest
1¹/₄ cups milk
1 egg, beaten
3 tablespoons virgin olive oil
2 tablespoons rolled oats
honey or maple syrup, to serve

1. Preheat the oven to 400°F. Put ten paper muffin cups into a muffin pan.

2. Sift the flour and baking powder into a bowl, adding any husks remaining in the strainer. Stir in the sugar and apricots.

3. Put the banana and orange juice into a separate bowl and mash. Add the orange zest, milk, egg, and oil, then mix well.

4. Make a well in the center of the flour mixture. Pour the banana mixture into the hole and mix well. Spoon the batter into the paper cups.

5. Sprinkle each muffin with a few rolled oats. Bake for 25–30 minutes, or until well risen and the tops spring back when pressed with a fingertip. Transfer to a wire rack. Serve warm, with a little honey or maple syrup.

WHEAT FLOUR
If you want to replace white flour with whole wheat flour in your recipes when baking at home, be sure to add a little more liquid.

PER MUFFIN: 173 CALS | 4.5G FAT | 0.7G SAT FAT | 25.6G CARBS | 9.5G SUGARS | 2G FIBER | 4.5G PROTEIN | 0.5G SALT

RASPBERRY RICOTTA CHEESECAKE

Traditionally, cheesecakes have a crushed cookie crust, but this granola-style crust is packed with protein-filled nuts and cholesterol-lowering oats.

SERVES: 8
PREP: 40 MINS   COOK: 15 MINS
SOAK: 5 MINS   CHILL: 6 HOURS

2 tablespoons unsalted butter
1 tablespoon virgin olive oil, plus extra to grease
1/3 cup maple syrup, plus extra to serve
1/2 cup rolled oats
1/2 cup coarsely chopped unblanched almonds
1/2 cup coarsely chopped unblanched hazelnuts

TOPPING
1/4 cup cold water
2 1/2 teaspoons powdered gelatin
1 cup ricotta cheese
1 cup mascarpone cheese
1 cup plain yogurt
finely grated zest and juice of 1 unwaxed lemon, plus extra zest to decorate
1 1/4 cups raspberries

1. To make the crust, preheat the oven to 325°F. Brush a 9-inch diameter round nonstick springform tart pan with a little oil. Put the butter, oil, and 2 tablespoons of maple syrup in a saucepan over medium-low heat until the butter has melted. Remove the pan from the heat and stir in the oats and nuts.

2. Transfer the mixture into the prepared pan and press down into an even layer with the back of a fork. Bake for 15 minutes, or until golden, then let cool.

3. To make the topping, spoon the water into a small heatproof bowl, then sprinkle the gelatin over the top, making sure all the powder is absorbed. Soak for 5 minutes. Place the bowl over a saucepan of gently simmering water until you have a clear liquid.

4. Put the ricotta, mascarpone, and yogurt in a bowl, spoon in the remaining 1/4 cup of maple syrup and beat until smooth. Mix in the lemon zest and juice, then gradually beat in the gelatin mixture. Add half the raspberries and crush them into the mixture with a fork.

5. Spoon the topping onto the crust and smooth the surface, then sprinkle with the remaining raspberries. Cover the cheesecake and chill in the refrigerator for 4–6 hours, or until set.

6. To serve, run a knife around the edge of the pan, release the side, and slide the cheesecake onto a serving plate. Decorate with the remaining lemon zest. To serve, cut into wedges and drizzle with extra maple syrup.

FREEZE IT
This cheesecake can be frozen for up to two months. Wrap the pan in plastic wrap, seal, and label. Defrost in the refrigerator for four hours, then for one hour at room temperature.

PER SERVING: 389 CALS | 29.3G FAT | 14.3G SAT FAT | 22.9G CARBS | 14.1G SUGARS | 3.2G FIBER | 11G PROTEIN | 0.2G SALT

HONEYED CARROT AND PECAN SQUARES

This cake is packed with vitamin A-boosting carrots, vitamin B- and mineral-boosting wheat germ, and energy-boosting whole wheat flour.

MAKES: 15 SQUARES
PREP: 25 MINS   COOK: 35 MINS

3 eggs
2/3 cup virgin olive oil
1/2 cup firmly packed light brown sugar
1/3 cup honey
1 1/3 cups whole wheat flour
1/4 cup wheat germ
2 teaspoons baking powder
2 teaspoons ground ginger
grated zest of 1 orange, plus extra to decorate
1 1/4 teaspoons ground allspice
1 1/2 cups shredded carrots
1/2 cup pecan pieces,
plus extra to decorate

FROSTING
1/2 plain Greek-style yogurt
2/3 cup cream cheese or mascarpone

1. Preheat the oven to 350°F. Line a nonstick 7 x 11–inch roasting pan with parchment paper, snipping into the corners diagonally, then pressing the paper into the pan so that both the bottom and sides are lined.

2. Crack the eggs into a large bowl, add the oil, sugar, and 1/4 cup of honey, and beat until smooth. Put the flour, wheat germ, and baking powder into a small bowl, then add the ginger, orange zest, and 1 teaspoon of allspice and stir. Add the dry ingredients to the egg batter and beat again until smooth. Add the carrots and pecans and stir.

3. Spoon the batter into the prepared pan and spread it into an even layer. Bake for 30–35 minutes, or until well risen and a toothpick comes out cleanly when inserted into the center of the cake.

4. Remove the cake from the pan, peel off the parchment paper, and turn out onto a wire rack. Let cool.

5. To make the frosting, put the yogurt, cream cheese, remaining 1 tablespoon of honey and 1/4 teaspoon of allspice in a bowl and beat together until smooth. Spread the frosting over the cake, then sprinkle with extra pecans and orange zest. Cut it into 15 squares and serve.

ALSO TRY
Use 2 coarsely grated raw beets
in place of the carrots.

PER SQUARE: 294 CALS | 20G FAT | 5.3G SAT FAT | 25.8G CARBS | 14.9G SUGARS | 2.4G FIBER | 5.3G PROTEIN | 0.5G SALT

GINGER, NUT, AND OAT COOKIES

Cookies warm from the oven make a great welcome for kids back from school or for guests. Keep the dough in the refrigerator and slice off cookies, then bake for 15 minutes.

MAKES: 18 BISCUITS
PREP: 30 MINS   CHILL: 30 MINS   COOK: 15 MINS

1½ sticks unsalted butter, softened and diced, plus extra to grease
½ cup firmly packed dark brown sugar
1-inch piece fresh ginger, peeled and finely chopped
1¼ cups whole wheat flour
1 cup rolled oats
¾ cup coarsely chopped unblanched hazelnuts
¾ cup coarsely chopped unblanched almonds

1. Place a sheet of parchment paper about 12 inches long on a work surface.

2. Cream together the butter, sugar, and ginger in a large bowl. Gradually beat in the flour, then the oats and nuts, until you have a soft dough. Spoon the dough into a 10-inch line along the parchment paper, then press it into a 2-inch diameter roll. Wrap in the paper and chill in the refrigerator for 30 minutes, or up to three days.

3. Preheat the oven to 350°F. Grease two baking sheets with butter. Unwrap the cookie dough and slice off as many cookies as you require. Arrange on the baking sheets, leaving a little space between each cookie. Bake for 12–15 minutes, or until cracked and browned at the edges.

4. Let the cookies cool for 5 minutes, then loosen them and transfer to a wire rack to cool completely.

ALSO TRY
Try these cookies with chopped semisweet chocolate or dates and finely grated orange zest instead of the ginger and chopped nuts.

PER COOKIE: 186 CALS | 12.7G FAT | 5.4G SAT FAT | 16.6G CARBS | 6.8G SUGARS | 2.2G FIBER | 2.3G PROTEIN | TRACE SALT

STUFFED NECTARINES

This indulgent-tasting summer dessert is packed with vitamin C and fiber, and takes just minutes to prepare.

SERVES: 4

PREP: 15 MINS   COOK: 10 MINS

¼ cup plain Greek-style yogurt
finely grated zest of ½ orange
4 ripe nectarines or peaches, halved and pitted
1 cup blueberries
1 cup raspberries
⅔ cup freshly squeezed orange juice
2 teaspoons honey
1 tablespoon brandy (optional)

1. Preheat the oven to 350°F. Put the yogurt and orange zest into a small bowl, cover, and chill in the refrigerator while you make the rest of the dessert.

2. Put the nectarines in a shallow ovenproof dish. Fill the hollows left by the removal of the nectarine pits with a mixture of blueberries and raspberries. Put any extra berries around the edge.

3. Put the orange juice, honey, and brandy, if using, in a small bowl, mix well, then pour the liquid over the fruit. Bake for 10 minutes, or until hot.

4. Serve immediately with the orange yogurt.

BUYING FRUIT

Avoid underripe nectarines, otherwise it will be difficult to remove the pits.

PER SERVING: 159 CALS | 2.7G FAT | 1.2G SAT FAT | 31.76 CARBS | 23G SUGARS | 5.4G FIBER | 3.2G PROTEIN | TRACE SALT

CRUSTED CINNAMON ORANGES

Halved oranges, topped with cinnamon and sugar, will smell delicious as they broil, and are a simple way to end a meal—or even for breakfast.

SERVES: 4

PREP: 5 MINS   COOK: 5 MINS

4 large oranges, halved and seeds discarded
1 teaspoon ground cinnamon
1 tablespoon packed light brown sugar

1. Preheat the broiler to high. Carefully cut the orange flesh away from the skin by cutting around the edge of the fruit with a sharp knife. Cut across the segments to loosen the flesh into bite-size pieces that will then spoon out easily.

2. Arrange the orange halves, cut side up, in a shallow, flameproof dish. Put the cinnamon and sugar into a small bowl, mix, then sprinkle the mixture over the oranges.

3. Broil for 3–5 minutes, or until the sugar has caramelized and is golden and bubbling. Serve immediately.

ALSO TRY
Top with plain yogurt mixed with honey for an extra-special treat.

PER SERVING: 88 CALS | 0.2G FAT | 0G SAT FAT | 20G CARBS | 20G SUGARS | 3.5G FIBER | 1.5G PROTEIN | TRACE SALT

SPICED PLUM AND BLACKBERRY BRULEES

A fresh, fruity compote lightly spiced with cinnamon, then topped with whipped cream and Greek-style yogurt for a no-bake brûlée custard—delicious!

SERVES: 6
PREP: 15 MINS   CHILL: 30 MINS   COOK: 15 MINS

5 plums, pitted and sliced
1¼ cups blackberries
2 tablespoons water
¼ teaspoon ground cinnamon
⅓ cup firmly packed light brown sugar
1 cup heavy cream
1 cup plain Greek-style yogurt

1. Put the plums, blackberries, and water into a saucepan, sprinkle with the cinnamon and 2 tablespoons of the sugar, then cover and cook over medium–low heat for 10 minutes, or until just tender. Let cool.

2. Put the cream in a large bowl and beat until soft swirls form, then fold in the yogurt.

3. Spoon the fruit and a little of the juice into six ovenproof ¾–cup ramekins or souffle dishes. Dot teaspoonfuls of the cream mixture over the top, then spread it into an even layer. Chill for at least 30 minutes.

4. Sprinkle the remaining 3 tablespoons of sugar over the tops of the dishes, then stand them in the bottom of the broiler pan, pack ice around them to keep them cold, and broil for 4–5 minutes, or until the sugar has dissolved and caramelized. Let cool for 2 minutes, then serve.

MAKE IT EASY
Caramelize the sugar at the very last minute with a cook's blowtorch instead of broiling.

PER SERVING: 310 CALS | 24G FAT | 15G SAT FAT | 21G CARBS | 21G SUGARS | 2.2G FIBER | 4.9G PROTEIN | TRACE SALT

MANGO FRUITY CRUSH ICE POPS

These three-layered fruity, creamy treats are packed with color, texture, and flavor. The mango and strawberries work hand in hand with the vanilla.

MAKES: 8 ICE POPS
PREP: 20 MINS   FREEZE: 8 HOURS

1 mango, peeled, pitted, and cubed
9 tablespoons honey
1¼ cups plain yogurt
2 teaspoons vanilla extract
2 cups hulled strawberry pieces

1. Put the mango in a blender or food processor and process to a puree. Transfer to a small bowl, add 3 tablespoons of honey, and stir well.

2. Pour the mixture into eight ½–cup ice pop molds. Freeze for 2 hours, or until firm.

3. When the mango mixture is frozen, put the yogurt, vanilla extract, and 3 tablespoons of honey in a bowl and stir well. Spoon it over the frozen mango mixture. Insert the ice pop sticks and freeze for 2–3 hours, or until firm.

4. When the vanilla mixture is frozen, put the strawberries and remaining 3 tablespoons of honey in a blender and process to a puree. Strain out the seeds with a fine metal strainer. Pour it over the frozen vanilla mixture and freeze for 2–3 hours, or until firm.

5. To unmold the ice pops, dip the frozen molds into warm water for a few seconds and gently release the ice pops while holding the sticks.

MMM, MANGO

Mangoes contain a selection of vitamins and minerals, and are particularly rich in vitamin C and betacarotene, which the body converts into vitamin A.

PER ICE POP: 141 CALS | 0.7G FAT | 0.3G SAT FAT | 33.3G CARBS | 31.7G SUGARS | 1.4G FIBER | 2.5G PROTEIN | TRACE SALT

INDEX

NOV _ 3 2016